Welcome to the Cheap Seats

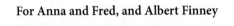

For Anna and Fred, and Albert Finney

Welcome to the Cheap Seats

Silver Screen Portrayals of the British Working Class

Andrew Graves

Five Leaves Publications

**Welcome to the Cheap Seats: Silver Screen Portrayals
of the British Working Class**
Andrew Graves

Published in 2019 by Five Leaves Publications
14a Long Row, Nottingham NG1 2DH
www.fiveleaves.co.uk
www.fiveleavesbookshop.co.uk

ISBN: 978-1-910170-62-5

Cover design by Richard Johnson

Printed in Great Britain

Contents

Acknowledgements

Thanks to Ross Bradshaw, William Ivory, Deirdre O'Neill, Lisa McKenzie, Caroline Hennigan, Broadway Cinema and Richard Johnson for your help, support and kind contributions.

Foreword
by Lisa McKenzie

If I let my imagination run away with me when I'm sat in what's left of the old pubs, with the big heavy wooden bars, fireplaces, and stools, or if I'm having a cuppa in a café, it's really easy to drift into black and white, and into a time when working-class people's lives, and accents, pubs, cafés, and workplaces could be seen in the cinema. Every year I go to the Goose Fair in Nottingham, and it never leaves me that this is the place where Arthur Seaton from Alan Sillitoe's *Saturday Night and Sunday Morning* rampaged and womanised. I know that I'm connected to something deeper and more important than my present, I'm connected to the ghosts of my working-class past, and they regularly haunt me. That haunting can sometimes be unsettling but mostly it's comforting.

The importance of a collection of working-class films, therefore, critiqued and remembered in this volume, should be obvious, so if it isn't, let me tell you just how important it is. I was raised on these films and they are as important and as much a part of my life as chips and egg and beans were for a Wednesday night tea, which was luxury bearing in mind it was mid-week, but Friday was the night I looked forward to all week.

Friday night my mum would get dressed up, she left the house to go to the Oval pub on our estate looking like Doreen from *Saturday Night and Sunday Morning*. The excitement for me as a child was when she came back, smelling like some other-worldly place that I desperately wanted to go to, this place had the best smell in the world, *Hartnell in Love* perfume and lager and lime and chips and vinegar. It hinted at other things beyond our front door, fantastic things, grown-up sparkly things. We sat together on the settee and watched the late film, eating our chips and cuddling and smiling. I was allowed to watch my mum's glamorous grown-up films. They weren't the Hollywood big budget musicals, they were always the British kitchen sink dramas. We watched *Saturday Night and Sunday Morning*, where my mum pointed out the Nottingham buses we used to get on to visit my auntie Annie. We laughed our heads off at *Billy Liar*; I didn't know what we were laughing at but I knew Billy was silly. At the end my mum used to have a tear in her eye, I never knew why.

We watched *A Kind of Loving*, and *A Taste of Honey*. I saw myself in those films, the children playing out on the streets, the ice cream vans, the skipping songs. I saw my family and my neighbours, I knew we were part of Britain, I knew I fitted somewhere.

When my mum had had a drink she was lovely, she cuddled me and kissed me, and squeezed me, and when the sad bits came on she squeezed my hands and said, 'Life is hard, it's always hard for us, but you have to hold your head up even when you are sad.' I watched Rita Tushingham holding her head up when she was sad, I watched Dora Bryan pull her shoulders back, and I watched Lynn Perry straighten the seams on her stockings, and I learned how to be a working-class woman from my mother and those films.

British working-class films are important, more important than we can really know, they are poignant, political, sometimes subtle, as in the beautiful *Kes*, and sometimes not. Sometimes they are a sledgehammer hitting you around the head — Arthur Seaton falling down the stairs blind drunk in the White Horse in Radford, or the closing, harrowing scene of *Cathy Come Home*, that even today I can't watch without a pain in my heart, still feeling my mum's arms hugging me. We both feared homelessness and, worst of all, being taken away from each other. This was entirely possible, as our situation was very similar to Cathy's.

These working-class stories are much more than stories, they connect us to our pasts, and they are important art forms for and by working-class people. They give a sense of what we are, and are our voices. They show we are part of this nation, we are valued. When working-class voices, stories and narratives are not told, or if they are only told by the middle classes, we are devalued, and class inequality and class prejudice continues. Working-class films, stories, narratives, art forms and poetry are the front line in fighting for class pride.

Read, and immerse yourself in this book, watch the films. When working-class people are disappearing from the public arena it is a political act to watch these films.

Lisa McKenzie is the author of *Getting By: Estates, Class and Culture in Austerity Britain*.

Introduction
Whatever You Say This Book Is,
That's What It's Not

I suppose if it were possible for this book to have a smell, other than the normal book smell, it would be the smell of the Mars Bars my dad bought for us on the way back from the pub on a Sunday afternoon. It would be his fading Brut aftershave, pervasive Brylcreem and second-hand Mansfield bitter breath. Smell is a powerful thing, it can transport us back through time. It was on those pungent Sunday afternoons of my childhood that I first came across some of those films that I have loosely placed into the category of 'working-class cinema'.

So, what do I mean by working-class cinema? Well, for the purposes of this book I am concentrating on feature films, not documentaries (though I will mention the odd documentary from time to time), and I am going to discuss a whole range of films which depict working-class people, families, groups or individuals. I shall examine films from the current era, the British New Wave of the early 60s and I will cast my net as far back as the silent age. Though it's a fairly long narrative which touches upon age, status, gender and race, it's essentially a book about people and the stories they tell via the medium of film.

I hope to capture my enthusiasm and love in sharing with you some of the delight, fascination and honest appreciation I have for these films. I will chart the rise and fall of the likes of Arthur Seaton and Billy Casper, and Combo from *This is England* and celebrate a side of British cinema that can be unflinching, aggressive, funny, joyous, brutal and heart-breaking. I will hopefully convince you that working-class cinema is not all about flat caps and whippets and black and white screens, that this story is a female story, a male story, a rich and colourful story encompassing culture and soul.

But be warned — this is not an academic study, nor is it a detailed historical document or a chronological guide to every single film which roughly falls into the category I have chosen to look at. This can only ever be a subjective viewpoint. There are many films which I have left out, for instance you won't find *Brassed Off* or *The Full Monty*, *Billy Elliot* or a host of other films up for discussion here. Sometimes it was because of time and space, sometimes it was because of personal choice and sometimes, God help me, they just didn't seem to fit the narrative. But I do believe the films I have included provide plenty of food for thought and allow me to examine topics like youth culture, criminality, immigration and censorship.

I hope reading this will reawaken your appetite for older classics like *Saturday Night and Sunday Morning*, *A Taste of Honey* and *Kes*, but I also hope that I will be able to tempt you with lesser-known gems such as *That Sinking Feeling*, *Babylon*, *Bronco Bullfrog* and *Jawbone*. I will also explore the lives and work of key players, whether they be actors, writers or directors, within this unique subset of British films, looking at the likes of Ken Loach, Mike Leigh, Shelagh Delaney, Andrea Dunbar and, of course, Albert Finney.

It's about the city, the rural and the run-down, it's about the factory, the pub and the kitchen sink. It's the grit and the glory and the kick in the teeth, it's the wondrous, the mundane, the salt in the wounds and the sugar in the tea. It's about the anger and the laughter, it's about injustice, love and hope.

Enjoy.

1. Suffer in Silence

We all want to help one another. Human beings are like that. We want to live by each other's happiness — not by each other's misery. We don't want to hate and despise one another. In this world, there's room for everyone and the good earth is rich and can provide for everyone.

The Great Dictator (1940)

There were only a few things guaranteed to drive me into a sulky, silent, doom-laden fit of despair when I was a child. One was the increasingly rational fear of looming all-out nuclear war, with its visions of mushroom clouds, radiation poisoning and its *Threads*-style battering of ugly, apocalyptic certainty. Another was having to watch my non-functional parents edge ever closer to that unspoken-of divorce that hovered on the horizon, waiting to pick the bones of our dying little family unit. But the overwhelming memory of dread I take with me from that era was supplied by the work of a recently-deceased ex-workhouse inmate from South London. His name was Charles Chaplin.

I think it began one rainy Saturday afternoon when I was fighting off the flu, blanket-bound on the settee, flanked by toilet rolls and Lucozade, and being force-fed rank-tasting Lemsip sachets by my overly busy mother, who thought the best way to get rid of a virus was to scowl at it every now and again. I was feeling sorry for myself in the way that only an eleven-year-old boy could. To cheer myself up, I switched on BBC2 for what the *Radio Times* had listed as a 'comedy film'.

Even taking into account the limited capabilities of our tiny, crappy Rediffusion telly, Charlie Chaplin's *Easy Street* (1917) felt a fairly bleak, unattractive affair. Comedy to me then was *On the Buses*, *Carry On* films, basically lots of leering, yellow-toothed hapless protagonists failing to chat up girls whilst falling on their arses. It was a Sid James cackle, an 'I'll get you Butler,' or a roller-skated Michael Crawford clinging desperately to the back of a red London bus. And while *Easy Street* had its fair share of pratfalls, it felt like a tainted form of slapstick, one framed with the brutality of an unnatural order, a mirth wrapped in the peeling dank of slum house industrial poverty, a black and white fever dream of lumbering, bushy-eyed bully boys and pinched and threadbare heroines. This was the world a dead clown was making me inhabit and I was too snotty and weak not to get caught up in his grim flickering spectre of a movie.

And if all this seems overly negative towards Chaplin, rest assured, thirty-odd years on, I stuck with him and now I would be the first to praise his work on a critical level and would certainly paint myself a fan of the 'Little Tramp'. And though I might laugh harder at Harold Lloyd, to give an obvious comparison, and feel a deeper love for Laurel and Hardy and Buster Keaton, Chaplin is the one that continues to fascinate and enlighten me. I suppose in some ways this opening chapter falls slightly outside the rest of this book, but I trust that this will be an important additional extra in that it offers a glimpse into the creative output of an inarguable genius who, for a time at least, managed to switch the Hollywood focus away from the glitz and glam and back onto the forgotten underclass and underdogs in a way that no other film-maker has since.

2016 will probably go down in history for the UK's decision to leave the EU, the American election of President Donald Trump and its high celebrity death count. But thirty-nine years previously, 1977 had been an equally cruel year for the famous and iconic. The film world alone saw the loss of legends like Joan Crawford, Bing Crosby, Elvis Presley, Groucho Marx, Delmer Daves, Howard Hawks, Jacques Tourneur, and Charlie Chaplin.

Though not the first movie star (Florence Lawrence, 'The Biograph Girl', arguably took that crown), Chaplin, as the Little Tramp, would take the idea of celebrity to a whole new level. For a while at least he was probably the most famous person in the Western world. His mere presence changed the way we saw motion pictures and engaged with the people that populated them. By 1915, Chaplin was such a hot property that a string of impersonators, including a bizarre female Chaplin, called Minerva Courtney, were able to make a living by openly stealing his act. A young Harold Lloyd made his early screen appearances as a character called Willie Work and later as Lucky Luke, both were thinly-veiled Chaplin rip-offs. The thievery continued unheeded until an ensuing court case deemed that the image of the Little Tramp belonged to Chaplin and Chaplin alone.

He made and starred in dozens of silent and sound pictures, a handful of which will go down in history as some of the best ever made. He also made enemies, largely because of his acknowledged communist sympathies and subversive screen messages. He was accused of being a foreign agent, trailed by the FBI and was effectively exiled from Hollywood and his adopted home country.

But his life began in a South London slum in the final decade of the nineteenth century. It was a shabby, dangerous and heartless world for a child, small for his age, to attempt to grow up in. Peter Ackroyd, in his excellent biography *Charlie Chaplin*, paints a lurid description of the young film-maker's early surroundings:

> It was in a sense cut off from the life of greater London; this may account for the air of exhaustion, and of torpor, which could hit the unwary. It was the site of small and noisome trades such as hat-making and leather tanning. Factories abounded for the manufacture of biscuits, jam and pickles. Glue factories stood adjacent to timber warehouses and slaughterhouses. The predominant smells were those of vinegar, and of dog dung and of smoke, and of beer, compounded of course by the stink of poverty.

Though Chaplin's male parentage remains unclear, the man who he himself referred to as father, in his entertaining, yet often-unreliable autobiography, was one Charles Chaplin senior. His 'father', often estranged from the family, was a crowd-pleasing music-hall entertainer, but as his popularity waned he seemed to spend more and more time in the bars of those establishments than he did on any stage. He died of alcohol-related illnesses when he was just thirty-eight. Chaplin junior's mother, Hannah, was also a music-hall entertainer and singer, but, according to most accounts, a faltering singing voice forced her out of show business and into the monotonous and penny-pinched life of a Dickensian seamstress. Hannah spent many of her remaining years in various mental institutions, her fragile state almost certainly made worse by the relentless grind of poverty, malnutrition and at least one recorded diagnosis of syphilis.

Not only were money and food usually scarce, so were other basics such as clothing. At one stage Charlie was made to suffer the indignity of having to wear his mother's cut-down old stage tights for socks. They were bright red and earned him the nickname Sir Walter Raleigh.

The beleaguered family unit, made up of Charlie, Hannah and Charlie's older brother, Sydney, also spent time in the workhouse. It was undoubtedly, by their own meagre standards and certainly by our modern sensibilities, a horrific and soul-destroying environment. Male and female residents were segregated, meaning the young Charlie was deprived of his mother's presence for weeks at a time. The aftermath of these formative and painfully-recalled early memories can perhaps be seen most clearly in his 1921 film *The Kid*, where the forced separation of a child and carer by a utilitarian and unemotional system is beautifully and heartbreakingly rendered. As an early film pioneer, he wasn't alone in living through extreme childhood conditions. His American contemporary, Buster Keaton, spent his formative years on stage playing a diminutive and seemingly indestructible human punchbag to his father's drunkenly ham-fisted vaudeville antics. The experience certainly didn't harm *his* future film career, but in the short term he was left illiterate and riddled with gonorrhoea by the age of sixteen.

Chaplin though, achieving the seemingly impossible, was able to wriggle away from the constraints of cruel and abject destitution, at first via the music-hall and stage — he was part of an unlikely clog-dancing troupe called The Eight Lancashire Lads, before landing a role in a production of *Sherlock Holmes*, which toured the provinces. His autobiography is filled with stories about his lonely and sometimes unsettling time on the road, with its bleak landladies, odd characters and unfamiliar settings, including this passage, describing his stay at a creepy lodging house in Wales, which reads more like the script for an early German Expressionist horror film than an actor's memoir:

> He led the way into the kitchen and rested the lamp on the dresser, which had a curtain strung across the bottom of it in place of cupboard doors. 'Hey Gilbert, come out of there!' he said, parting the curtains.
>
> A half man with no legs, an oversized, blond, flat-shaped head, a sickening white face, a sunken nose, a large mouth and powerful muscular shoulders and arms, crawled from underneath the dresser. He wore flannel underwear with the legs of the garment cut to the thighs, from which ten thick, stubby toes stuck out. The grisly creature could have been twenty or forty. He looked up and grinned, showing a set of yellow, widely-spaced teeth.

Eventually, alongside Sydney, Chaplin became part of the famous Fred Karno Circus. It was during his time with Karno (who at first hardly reckoned the underdeveloped interloper) that the young performer really began to develop his comedic chops. He quickly became the star of the show, his party piece being a worse-for-wear character dubbed 'The Inebriated Swell' in a sketch called *The Mumming Birds*.

A tour of Paris ensued, as did a tour of the US where his roommate and understudy was one Arthur Stanley Jefferson, who would later become Stan Laurel. It was in America where Chaplin was first spotted in 1913 by a talent scout from Max Sennett's burgeoning film studio The Keystone Film Company.

Much has been said about Chaplin's rise to world stardom, his unfortunate relationships with *much* younger women, his marriage breakups, the subsequent court case where he faced an indictment under the Mann Act (the White-Slave Traffic Act of 1910), and his decline at the hands of a changing popular culture and J. Edgar Hoover and the FBI, but in keeping with the context of this book, I wanted to concentrate on his film output and his significance in the pantheon of what I have loosely described as working-class cinema.

Many critics point to Chaplin's mid-career pictures from 1921's *The Kid* through to *The Great Dictator* (1940) as his most culturally significant, rebellious and engaging films, and this is for good reason. I will be coming to some of those releases shortly, but it's worth going back to examine some of his early works and in particular to look at the importance of the Little Tramp.

In 1913, the same year Chaplin signed his first motion picture deal, the world was just months away from war, in the UK the age of automatic deference was on its last legs, Russia grumbled ever closer to all-out revolution and in America, now Chaplin's adopted home country, citizens were beginning to feel the effects of a sharp unprecedented recession. This kick-started a wave of organised demonstrations, strikes and boycotts, often led by the Industrial Workers of the World. Violence and arrests often ensued. Unemployment and poverty were on the rise.

In his autobiography, Chaplin describes the way he came about his famous image in the flowing passage:

> ... I thought I would dress in baggy pants, big shoes, a cane and a derby hat. I wanted everything a contradiction: the pants baggy, the coat tight, the hat small, the shoes large ... I added a small moustache, which, I reasoned would add age without hiding my expression ... I had no idea of the character ... I began to know him and by the time I walked onto the stage he was fully born.

This version of the story is most likely a simplification of the genesis of the famous image and the reality was it was probably much less contrived and was just as likely to be the result of a poorly-equipped costume wardrobe and breakneck-speed production, which left little room for political delineation; but whichever way Chaplin's bowler-hatted cane-carrying character came in to being (and there is significant disagreement on this), it become a potent and timely symbol, as discussed during the Charlie Chaplin episode of Radio 4's *The Mark Steel Lecture*.

> ... and in America a major symbol of opposition to the factory system was the image of the tramp. In February 1914, a mob of seven hundred tramps burst into a church in Manhattan demanding food and shelter and a mass rally of the Industrial Workers of the World supported them, they urged them to occupy churches throughout America. One of the most popular songs of the time was one that began 'Hallelujah, I'm a bum' ...

Many of his early 'Tramp' films may have been cruder and less nuanced than his later, more painstaking productions, when he had progressed from mere clown to full-blown auteur, but from the beginning there was an effort to present us with comedy, yes, but a comedy only thinly disguising a more subversive social message, often told from the point of view of the underdog or the 'little man'. By the time he had switched studios from Keystone to Essanay in 1915, it was clear that the character of the Tramp was beginning to move away from the more restrictive slapstick-driven simpleton, that he was starting to feel hampered under the uneasy gaze of a metaphorical one-way street, Max Sennett. Films like *The Bank* (1915) and *The Tramp* (1915), were important turning points for Chaplin, the use of romance and pathos helped solidify the character's appeal both artistically and critically. A key moment comes at the end of *The Tramp*, Chaplin walks sadly away into the distance but before the final fade out he pulls himself together and totters away into the sunset, the picture of health and happiness. It was a visual trope that we would link forever with Chaplin and would be repeated, most notably in his masterpiece *Modern Times* (1936), with a beautifully-ragged Paulette Goddard in tow.

His time spent with the Mutual Film Company, which he often cited as being the happiest of his career, saw his work develop further and a flurry of critically-acclaimed two-reelers ensued. Often these films would reflect more of the 'working-class experience' than other contemporary efforts, or at the very least the humble existence of the wage slave, public servant or foreign migrant. Features like *The Floorwalker* (1916), *The Fireman* (1916) and *The Immigrant* (1917) present us not just with comedic bits of business, though there are many highlights of this nature, particularly in *The Pawnshop* (1916), with its dizzying mix of slapstick and absurdity, but also with a dour, damp monochrome shabbiness. It's as though the charm and hilarity of these films are not enough to keep out the encroaching reality of a world in which many were suffering, hidden in the poverty-stricken shadows where most burgeoning Hollywood pictures would refuse to go.

And it's with *Easy Street* (1917) that we see a distinctly more autobiographical and rebellious Chaplin at play, as though away from the world-wide stardom, glamour and celebrity, his humblest of beginnings were finally catching up with him in this funny yet bleak black and white ballet of pratfalls and prototype social realism. The street scenes could have been lifted from his own childhood slum memories and the conditions which rot away at the edges of the laughter are a stark reminder of the inequality of a rigged system which lurked uncomfortably just yards away from the packed movie houses. The film manages to satirise subtly (and not so subtly) the sanctimony and hypocrisy of a church whose willing collusion with a state whose inability or refusal to address a worsening situation only compounds the ills it preaches against. The story's central premise too is one of great political irony, in that the Little Tramp is driven so far to the edges of society by a system which seems designed to create swathes of poverty that the only way he can survive is to join the police force, thus becoming an enforcing member of the destructive state's wealth-driven armoury.

1921's *The Kid* is easily the film-maker's most emotional piece and possibly one of his angriest, harking back as it does to his own boyhood recollection when he, like the screaming Jackie Coogan in the title role, was ripped away from the arms of his parent by a social care system that treated the poor as little more than criminals or animals.

In 1919, Chaplin, alongside partners Douglas Fairbanks, Mary Pickford and D.W. Griffith, formed United Artists, a brand new distribution company. This freed Chaplin from the constraints of what would later become the so-called 'star system', ostensibly a means for studios to groom and control their contract players. It was a system which led to the undoing of many a star and often left writers and directors with little to do other than toe an increasingly hypocritical, corporate line. It saw off emotionally damaged Jean Harlow, and all-too-homosexual William Haines, and even propped up the faltering reputation of accused rapist Errol Flynn. But with United Artists, Chaplin at least could flourish artistically. The move also led to him being treated to further scrutiny by establishment figures, who perhaps realised what they feared most of all was a subversive film-maker who now owned the means for his own production.

The next decade or so saw Chaplin release some of the most acclaimed features of his career, including *The Gold Rush* (1925), *The Circus* (1928) and *City Lights* (1931). The latter was a wonderfully sad, funny and well-aimed pot-shot at American city living and the hypocrisies therein. Coinciding with the start of the Great Depression and its devastating social effects, the widening gap between the super-wealthy and the forgotten working class is sharply observed in this 'comedy romance in pantomime', as the opening credits remind us. At the beginning of the film, we home in on a public statue unveiling, but the important dignitaries on hand to deliver speeches are given a swift satirical kick in the pants the moment they open their mouths. Chaplin removes their dignified status, only allowing these characters to speak in Punch and Judy style squawks and squeaks. The pomposity of the rich and powerful is pricked within the first few seconds of the action.

Shortly after this the sheet from the new statue is removed revealing Chaplin's sleeping tramp in the arms of one of the impressive-looking sculptures. When a policeman screams at the tramp to move out of the way, Chaplin pauses by the outstretched fingers of one of the statue's huge hands. The fingers seem to rest on his nose, giving the none-too-subtle impression that Chaplin is thumbing his nose at authority.

The film, which features the first of many musical scores written by Chaplin himself, also skilfully plays with the idea of seeing and perception. It particularly picks apart the way that many within society view wealth or poverty and the people who choose to, or who are forced to exist within the means of those very different aspects of modern living. Towards the beginning of the film and again at the end the tramp is cruelly teased by a couple of kids, who can only 'see' him as a figure of ridicule, someone who inhabits the very bottom of society, thus affording him no respect. Then there is the rich socialite, who is rescued by the tramp from his own attempted suicide. He can only 'see' the tramp as a human being and equal when he is blind drunk. The moment he sobers up and can 'see' again, the tramp is cast out of his life. The blind flower girl (Virginia Cherrill) offers us more hope though. At first she projects her own ideas of personality and value onto the figure of the tramp, largely due to a comic misunderstanding. She spends most of the film believing the tramp to be a rich benefactor, and when she finally is able to see him due to a life-changing operation, we are left hoping that she will accept him for who he is. But as the film closes on this scene, we will never know, ending as it does on a close shot of Chaplin, his face aching with both joy and a growing fear that he may once again be rejected. The flower motif used in the film has valuable symbolic significance, as it is a temporary distraction which will eventually rot away. It is this idea of transience which lurks at the heart of the film, that all things will come to pass, be they superficial attachments or deeply ingrained (and unequal) political systems.

City Lights has much to say about inequality and the distorted values we place on the more materialistic aspects of life such as big cars, fashionable clothing and the desire to be 'seen' in the right places, but it also reminds us of our need for actual substance (no matter how transient those qualities turn out to be) by means of friendship, love and understanding.

And if the film was unconventional in terms of its subject matter and its much-discussed 'anti-capitalist' sentiment, its technical aspects equally flew in the face of the acceptable. In 1927, the first 'talking picture', *The Jazz Singer*, starring Al Jolson, was released and by 1931, sound productions were the norm, so *City Lights* is ostensibly a silent film release at a time when silent features (alongside many of the people who had become stars because of them), were being put out to pasture. It is testament to either Chaplin's stubbornness or his tenacity. However, even Chaplin's resolve was shaken when the film performed poorly at a preview in Los Angeles. Thankfully, due to the director's canny ability for garnering publicity and generating public attention via an increased promotional budget, *City Lights* went on to be a financial success.

But it's with *Modern Times* (1936) where Chaplin, already monitored closely by the FBI for his perceived communist allegiances, would succeed in creating one of the most subversive and anti-establishment

Hollywood films of the early twentieth century. He recalled his initial inspirations for making the film in his autobiography:

> Then I remembered an interview I had had with a bright young reporter on the *New York World*. Hearing that I was visiting Detroit, he had told me of the factory-belt system there — a harrowing story of big industry luring healthy young men off the farms who, after four or five years at the belt system, became nervous wrecks.

The first thing we see in *Modern Times* is a clock. The second hand moves quickly and menacingly about the art deco timepiece as the credits appear and a noisily constructed orchestral stab, a musical version of the factory siren, wakes us from our daydreams. It's time for work. We cut to a shot of herded sheep which quickly dissolves into a scene of city workers rammed against each other in the Bedlam-like morning rush to ride the subway to the nightmarish conveyor belts which await. We are quickly introduced to the Kafkaesque environment of the factory floor, where slave-driving bosses appear, like Big Brother, on huge monitor screens to castigate lack of productivity and rage at the criminality of over-long toilet breaks. We see a young worker being unwillingly served food by a time-saving device, which mirrors, albeit comically, the disturbing Ludovico scene from Kubrick's later *A Clockwork Orange* (1971), and in one cinematically iconic moment, the Little Tramp is fed into the machine, in a beautifully rendered yet scarily symbolic attack on a psychotic form of ever-hungry capitalism.

Also in the film, we are introduced to the skin and bones beauty of the urchin-like Paulette Goddard. When we first meet her, billed only as 'A Gamin' we gatecrash into her pathetic and motherless family setup, one ravaged by the mass unemployment which envelops their grim industrial environment. When her father is killed at an unemployed workers' rally, she is left orphaned and narrowly escapes being taken into care, where her younger sisters already are. Forced to survive on her wits and petty thievery, it is at that stage she first meets the tramp. Later, after escaping from a paddy wagon, the pair set up home together, no more than a chaotic, half-collapsing shack on the edge of town, a harsh metaphorical reminder of where 'decent society' places them — a problem best forgotten about. Although the shack setup supplies us with some of the most touching scenes of the film, it also offers us something much more tragic. That two people should have been challenged so cruelly by a morally bankrupt system, that they have grown to accept their ramshackle existence, with its scraps of food and little else, is deeply disturbing and Chaplin at his subversive best.

And while *City Lights* may have been more prettily composed, *The Circus* funnier and *Monsieur Verdoux* (1947) more controversial, *Modern Times* will forever be his quick-witted, clowning glory, a kick in the bollocks to a two-faced and immoral establishment. An establishment that panicked when Chaplin, the very embodiment of the American Dream they glorified — a poor immigrant made good — turned out to have a social conscience.

On September 19 1952, the day after he left New York to embark on a European trip to promote his latest film, *Limelight*, the then Attorney General James P. McGranery decided to revoke Chaplin's US re-entry permit (Chaplin had never actually become an American citizen). This meant that he would have had to submit to a formal interview about his 'moral behaviour' and political views before they would consider letting him back into the country. A few years earlier he had been served a subpoena to appear before the House Un-American Activities Committee, and while he was never called (perhaps because he threatened to appear dressed as the Tramp), this constant hounding was probably the reason he decided not to attempt re-entry. He later said of his experiences: 'Whether I re-entered that unhappy country or not was of little consequence to me. I would like to have told them that the sooner I was rid of that hate-beleaguered atmosphere the better, that I was fed up of America's insults and moral pomposity...'

While he was far from perfect as a human being, it seems doubtful that he deserved the public battering he received at the hands of J. Edgar Hoover and the FBI, and his subsequent 'unofficial' exile from the United States could have only felt to him like bitter overkill.

It's easy to forget just how many times Chaplin was on the right side of history — he was publicly anti-Hitler, with his film *The Great Dictator*, at a time when America and many other countries were still very much following the route of appeasement. Hollywood, having become a home to many European exiles, was unwilling to rattle the cage of the Austrian-born megalomaniac. Many studios took the line that any criticism they supported could make it worse for the people still living there. Chaplin's own response was 'Worse? How could it be any worse?'

He was also quick to document, through the means of comedy and the developing moving picture industry, the lot of the impoverished masses, the inequalities and hypocrisies of big city living, and he was unafraid to speak up off-screen about a range of social ills and problems.

His much-touted swan-song, *The Freak*, about a South American girl who sprouts wings and is captured and exhibited as an anomaly, possibly would have reflected his own dealings with fame, the media and the establishment, but as the film was never made, we will never know for sure.

On Christmas Day 1977, Chaplin died of a stroke in his bed; he was eighty-eight. Even after his death there was controversy. In 1978, in a bizarrely Chaplinesque set up, his body was dug up and held to ransom by two unemployed Polish immigrants. It was later recovered but the whole sorry episode played out with the grisly humour of a *Monsieur Verdoux*-style black comedy.

To some, Chaplin is a long-forgotten screen image, a bowler-hatted silhouette or a hastily put together fancy dress afterthought. To most he is a silent star from the golden age, a black and white Athena poster, a funny man with a Hitler moustache who once made some films. He is also a contradiction, a man of the people and a very private figure, a rich man and an anti-capitalist, an artist and a tyrant both shy and egocentric. To me, though, he will always be a rebel, the important kind of rebel, not the trendy designer agitator of celebrity cocktail parties, but the kind of provocateur who was faced with jail, lawsuits, exile and worse, who still managed to stick to his principles and make some of the most enduring screen images the world has ever seen.

> Whatever were my ill vicissitudes, I believe that fortune and ill fortune drift upon one haphazardly as clouds. Knowing this, I am agreeably surprised at the good. I have no design for living, no philosophy — whether sage or fool, we must all struggle with life. I vacillate with inconsistencies; at times, small things will annoy me and catastrophes will leave me indifferent.
>
> Charlie Chaplin

2: Dole Cues

On the outskirts of every city, there is a region of darkness and
poverty where men and women forever strive to live decently in
the face of overwhelming odds...

Love on the Dole (1941)

Almost a full year before Charlie Chaplin signed his first motion picture deal with Max Sennett's Keystone Film Company, the *Daily Mail* was getting jittery about Jesus. To be more precise, it was getting jittery over the cinematic portrayal of Jesus. On October 3 1912, *From the Manger to the Cross*, an early American biblical biopic directed by Sidney Olcott, began its eight-month run at the Queen's Hall theatre in London. Though the film was critically well-received and an invited group of clergymen could find no air of blasphemy or controversy about the production, the *Daily Mail* was not so satisfied. 'Is nothing sacred to the film-maker?' they cried indignantly, and kicked up much fuss about the sum of Judas-style silver pieces that film studio Kalem (quickly bought out by Vitograph) would make from this ungodly American abomination. The short version of this story is that the resultant media strop forced the Kinematograph Manufacturers Association and the Cinematograph Exhibitors Association to form a joint committee in 1912, which in turn would form a self-regulatory body called the British Board of Film Censors (BBFC), in an effort to ward off stricter controls from outside forces.

According to the Tom Dewe Mathews book *Censored*, the brand-new organisation would work something like this:

> The board would be set up by the industry itself: it would be financed by the fees paid by producers seeking a 'Certificate' from the Board, thereby avoiding the need for public funds; but the Board would be under the leadership of a Home Office appointed chief censor who would in turn act as an arbiter between the new Board and film-makers unwilling to accept its decisions. The deputation also conceded that the chief censor's rulings would be final and, even more crucially, that there would be no means of appeal against his decisions.

Ironically, or fittingly depending on your point of view, given that the formation of the Board was due largely to (albeit slightly dubious) religious outrage, this kind of system borrowed heavily from the papal 'Index' of censorship formalised by the Vatican secretariat during the sixteenth century in an effort to ward off Protestant reformation.

But it's the nature of censorship and government, and other official interference with the British film industry's output and how that affected early portrayals of the working classes, that I want to look at in this chapter. To do that we need to go back to the very beginnings of cinematic history.

Not satisfied with illuminating and enriching our lives by unleashing on the world such inventions as the light bulb and the gramophone, Thomas A. Edison also sought to corrupt the souls of the lower orders. At least, that was the view espoused by many a member of polite Edwardian society. It was his patented Kinetoscope which seemed to stiffen their collars. Better known as peepshows, flickers or 'What the Butler Saw Machines', these fairground attractions, little boxes of sin, fed with salacious-sounding productions like *Beware my Husband Comes*, *Seminary Girls*, or my particular favourite, *Love in a Hammock*, proved to be popular with a beleaguered working class, looking for a brief escape from an arduous existence.

And there was the problem, according to certain sections of the upper echelons. It was a pastime which they felt themselves above, a squalid thing of miserable undeserved and uncultured recreation and as it was something the proletariat could glean enjoyment from, they immediately sought to ban or control it.

But as with all new technologies, there is often an interval between its inception and its rise in popularity, and this interval can sometimes create a period of perceived lawlessness. Despite concerns raised by the state and the church there was little initially, at least legally, anyone could do to curtail what many saw as a burgeoning means of corruption amongst the great unwashed.

Even when film spilled out of the confines of the Kinetoscopes and onto makeshift screens, when the first projected productions were shown at the very end of the nineteenth century, control or censorship in the UK, at least in any organised nationally recognised sense, failed to materialise. The only film to be withdrawn in this era was not one of the more risqué titles such as *How Bridget Served the Salad Undressed*, or *Girl Climbing a Tree*, or *Cockfight*, but a short documentary-style piece detailing the production of Stilton. It was the detailed, microscopic glimpse into the bacterial world which existed below the surface of this delicious dairy product which really landed the 1898 film in hot water. It was possibly the first example of corporate interference, and it shows us that in those days the promise of naked girls, animal exploitation or violence wasn't enough to garner protest, but upsetting the UK's cheese industry definitely was.

It's easy to forget just how comfortable our twenty-first century cinema-going trips are. Aside from the odd rustle of sweet wrappers or the annoying instances of mid-feature mobile phone use, we can enjoy a stress-free film-viewing experience. Even if that all gets too much, we can always choose to stay within the comfort of our living rooms and watch something on one of the various forms of media streaming devices which are now part and parcel of our lives. But just imagine the experience of the thousands of working-class patrons who would regularly cram into the pre-theatre setups of the early twentieth century. Film shows or 'penny gaffs' were often exhibited in hurriedly-converted shops or other such abandoned buildings. They were poorly equipped, cramped, and conditions were squalid. Rudimentary films would be projected either straight onto whitewashed walls or onto a stretched canvas. The evening's entertainment would be played out in complete darkness, as no side lights were installed. Customers were so packed in and so transfixed by the images projected before them that there were many cases of people, both male and female, relieving themselves on the spot. Subsequently, early picture houses would reek of urine, sweat, smoke and, if they were a more reputable place, disinfectant. The complete blackness would not only provide cover for certain forms of more intimate behaviour but it was also the cause of minor accidents. This, coupled with the poor ventilation and fire risk, eventually led to the first victory for an outraged moral minority.

The poor conditions of most penny gaff establishments led well-meaning social reformers to campaign for more suitable, custom-built venues, and while the general desire for more adequately-equipped picture houses was on the whole a positive thing, one has to wonder why those same largely upper-middle-class social reformers weren't also paying more attention to the appalling housing conditions and workspaces which the average patron of the penny gaff was forced to endure.

Whatever the intentions, the result was the Government's introduction of the 1909 Cinematograph Act. The Act, according to the British Film Institute, 'was designed to regulate public screenings of films and to ensure that cinemas were in a suitable physical state to screen films safely. The Act was created in the first place because highly unstable nitrate film stock had caused several serious fires.'

While this all sounds like sensible health and safety regulation, the problems began when overzealous local authorities, spurred on by parsons, teachers and civic leaders, used the vague wording of the Act to justify their own sense of ethical and or religious outrage. The Act's use of the term 'inflammable film' for example, was interpreted by many councils as an excuse not to just deal physically with the potential mishandling of volatile nitrate reels, which may cause fires, but also to tackle any 'inflammable film' *content* to which they objected on moral grounds.

The Act itself made no reference whatsoever to the content of films — it was essentially an early piece of safety legislation — but it led to many local authorities drawing up their own list of guidelines for individual exhibitors to abide by. As different councils and authorities would predictably have their own ideas about what was acceptable, this meant films might be allowed in one area but not in another. This sent many an exhibitor into a fit of frustration, reeling in the wake of the Act's chaotic implications.

Also, around this time, partly because the Act demanded more suitable venues to exhibit film shows, and partly because there was a desire for the industry to attract the more lucrative middle-class demographic, there was a push by exhibitors to move the film shows from the grotty, cramped penny gaffs and into venues more acceptable to the moneyed-up bourgeoisie.

At first, there was an attempt to lure the middle classes into the music-halls, where short films were already being shown between the live performances, but often the films were so amateurish and pedestrian that even by the standards of the day they came across as little more than badly-made home movies. But, gradually, custom-built theatres began to appear. In 1907 there were around 250 venues, and just four years later there were over 4000. Unlike the penny gaffs, these establishments were plush, beautifully-decorated, staffed by uniformed workers and managers, and were seen as being much more suitable surroundings for the 'more respectable' middle class.

Not surprisingly, once more middle-class elements of society began to frequent the newly-built Empires, Majestics or Jewels, there was initially a resentment that the working classes were allowed to view entertainment in the same establishments (albeit in much cheaper seats). In some areas concerns were raised and there were even suggestions that the less well-at-heel should be made to use different entrances and exits so as not to embarrass the more affluent clientele.

Thankfully, objections like these were short-lived and soon the new 'cinemas' became relatively class-free environments, where patrons, regardless of their background, could, for the price of a ticket, enjoy the miracle of the modern picture palace in all its flickering glory. But the introduction of the BBFC in 1912 began to create discrepancies in the ways in which the classes were treated, not in the foyers of picture houses, but on the silver screens themselves.

Films swiftly moved from the quickie, unedited, jerky and amateurish productions of the peepshows and penny gaffs into much more creative areas. The cinematic art form began to flourish. In the years immediately preceding and following the Great War, the world's cinema-goers were introduced to the work of Charlie Chaplin, D.W. Griffith and Cecil B. DeMille. They thrilled to the onscreen exploits of iconic film characters like Mary Pickford and Rudolph Valentino, and revelled in the exotic beauty of prototype goth vampire Theda Bara. Europe, particularly Germany, became an imaginative hotbed for resourceful and innovative directors. It introduced a curious public to the visually stunning and nightmarish landscapes of Expressionist features such as *The Cabinet of Doctor Caligari* (1920) and *Nosferatu* (1922), letting us know that the film world had quickly found its feet and also its teeth. There were wonders to behold at any one of the thousands of picture palaces which now dominated the high streets of every town and city across the UK.

And yet, no sooner had this modern mode of entertainment established itself as an accepted amusement for all classes of citizen, there came a creeping desire from certain quarters to introduce new measures of control and conformity. Ever wary of an increasingly politically savvy proletariat, the UK establishment began to lean heavily on this potentially subversive new art form, to ensure it remained loyal to King and country and, more importantly, that it was seen to hold no truck with radicals, freethinkers and potential revolutionaries.

First of all, I think we need to underline the fact that until its change in focus in 1984, the BBFC stood for the British Board of Film *Censors*, not the British Board of Film *Classification*. And while some would argue that classification is just another version of censorship, I think that even the most hardened of libertines might concede that there is perhaps room for basic age classification in terms of cinema-going. I mean, who wants their seven-year-old watching *The Human Centipede*? (Whether this is enforceable in a smartphone/internet age is another issue.) But with actual censorship in its truest form, it's important to examine the nature of that censorship and the reasoning behind it in terms of class and establishment. The question we need to ask is not who early film censors were trying to protect, but who they were trying to silence and placate.

While the liberal part of me is knee-jerkingly opposed to censorship, even I would have to admit that at certain points in history, art, whether it be film, literature or whatever, has often been improved when forced to run the rigour of preconceived restriction. The argument is that in those circumstances, film-makers, writers or artists are being given a bigger target at which to aim their more carefully-honed levels of satire or subversion. Now, don't get me wrong, I am not advocating book burning for the sake of improving the subtext-devising skills of beleaguered creatives, but if we take a movie like James Whales' *Bride of Frankenstein* (1935) for instance, a film which was released and made under the strictest form of American film censorship, the Hays Code, it still manages to present us with an anti-establishment rebellious and wildly camp piece of early horror, incorporating references to necrophilia, grave-robbing and Christian blasphemy, in an era in which even innocuous on-screen behaviour like an over-long heterosexual kiss was baulked at. Arguably, the artistry at play in *Bride of Frankenstein* is better because it was made in a period of restriction and not liberation.

But putting aside the ability of certain directors to pull the wool over the eyes of many an obtuse film censor, the original intentions of the BBFC need to be examined in order to show how their questionable early rules and guidelines proved to be another tool in the establishment's armoury to keep the working class in its place.

The BBFC first started its operations on January 1 1913, based at 75 Shaftesbury Avenue. Their initial President and Chief Censor was George A. Redford. Though he had no formal experience in movie production, he had been the Chief Examiner of Plays under the Lord Chamberlain, much to the disapproval of playwright George Bernard Shaw, who had his own convoluted and contradictory thoughts on censorship. Aside from launching various campaigns which rallied against censorship, Shaw also argued that censorship was necessary for the 'uneducated majority'. Redford, though, soon became too ill to carry out his role other than in name only. The bulk of his work was transferred to the then BBFC Secretary, Joseph Brooke Wilkinson.

Whatever we think now about Wilkinson's handling of his position, it's clear that his role was unenviably difficult. Not only was he courting the wrath of the film industry, he also had to try and placate the political right and left, the military, religious groups and local councils. On top of this he was going blind.

Originally, the BBFC only had two actual rules when it came to what could and couldn't be included in a particular film, these were: no depictions or 'materialisations' of Christ, and no nudity. In terms of classification, films were divided into 'U' which meant largely, as it does today, that the film was deemed okay for all audiences, and 'A' which was a little like our 'PG' rating today, while under-sixteens were advised not to see such films, they could not be barred from doing so. Over time its list of restrictions would grow. In its first year 166 films were objected to. Of those 144 had to be recut and the rest were banned.

You can imagine the film industry's consternation. They had initially suggested setting up the BBFC in order to avoid all kinds of arbitrary and unsophisticated censure, but now they were faced with even greater disapproval. Like the protagonist of *Bride of Frankenstein*, they had created a monster.

Though the film censor's recommendations could be overturned by local councils, most authorities welcomed the BBFC's more draconian approach, some banning films even when they had been passed by Redford and Co.

It was soon felt that as with the initial introduction of the Cinematograph Act of 1909, the level of inconsistency from place to place was making a mockery of the proposed system. For a while it was touted by not only the film industry but many of the local councils that there should be a central government-controlled board of censors that would effectively trump the authority of the BBFC. This was compounded by the fact that there was a growing concern that there was a direct link between juvenile delinquency and cinema-going. In 1917, a public enquiry was carried out into the cinema with 'particular reference to young people' by the National Council of Public Morals, essentially an umbrella organisation for a host of moral reform groups. The report eventually dismissed the idea that that responsibility for juvenile delinquency could be placed solely at the feet of the film world and the industry was dealt a much more favourable hand than it had been before. This was in part to do with the contributions of T.P. O'Connor, the BBFC's successor to George A. Redford. Based on the Board's Annual Reports from 1913–1915, he instigated a new policy listing forty-three grounds for deletion and censorship. It was a move that set out to prove the 'strictness' of the new Board and to appease the many groups and moral reformers they needed to keep on side if the organisation were to survive.

The list of prohibited themes ran as follows:

1. Indecorous, ambiguous and irreverent titles and subtitles
2. Cruelty to animals
3. The irreverent treatment of sacred subjects
4. Drunken scenes carried to excess
5. Vulgar accessories in the staging
6. The *modus operandi* of criminals
7. Cruelty to young infants and excessive cruelty and torture to adults, especially women
8. Unnecessary exhibition of under-clothing
9. The exhibition of profuse bleeding
10. Nude figures
11. Offensive vulgarity, and impropriety in conduct and dress
12. Indecorous dancing
13. Excessively passionate love scenes
14. Bathing scenes passing the limits of propriety
15. References to controversial politics
16. Relations of capital and labour
17. Scenes tending to disparage public characters and institutions
18. Realistic horrors of warfare
19. Scenes and incidents calculated to afford information to the enemy
20. Incidents having a tendency to disparage our Allies
21. Scenes holding up the King's uniform to contempt or ridicule
22. Subjects dealing with India, in which British Officers are seen in an odious light, and otherwise attempting to suggest the disloyalty of British Officers, Native States or bringing into disrepute British prestige in the Empire
23. The exploitation of tragic incidents of the war
24. Gruesome murders and strangulation scenes
25. Executions

26. The effects of vitriol throwing
27. The drug habit. e.g. opium, morphia, cocaine, etc.
28. Subjects dealing with White Slave traffic
29. Subjects dealing with premeditated seduction of girls
30. 'First Night' scenes
31. Scenes suggestive of immorality
32. Indelicate sexual situations
33. Situations accentuating delicate marital relations
34. Men and women in bed together
35. Illicit relationships
36. Prostitution and procuration
37. Incidents indicating the actual perpetration of criminal assaults on women
38. Scenes depicting the effect of venereal disease, inherited or acquired
39. Incidents suggestive of incestuous relations
40. Themes and references relative to 'race suicide'
41. Confinements
42. Scenes laid in disorderly houses
43. Materialisation of the conventional figure of Christ

Many items on the list are not surprising, given that it was drawn up in the early Edwardian era, a time when public exhibitions of love-making were still frowned upon, and the public, already in the midst of a bloody world conflict, were not ready to be shown 'realistic horrors of warfare'. But there are other items on the list that seem to move away from mere prudishness or squeamishness and stray into the area of a more biased political agenda.

Items 15 (references to controversial politics), 16 (relations of capital and labour) and 17 (scenes tending to disparage public characters and institutions), would certainly play a useful role when it came the outright UK banning of the Russian film and critically acclaimed classic, *Battleship Potemkin* (1925). Eisenstein's film has been praised repeatedly over the years for its ground-breaking use of montage. Orson Welles, Michael Mann and many others have spoken favourably about the piece and Billy Wilder described it as his 'favourite film of all time'. It tells the tale of a beleaguered and downtrodden battleship crew who are driven to mutiny in the face of the inhuman on-board conditions in which they are being forced to exist. It contains one of the most famous scenes ever filmed, 'The Odessa Steps' sequence, and is a powerfully rendered, beautifully photographed pro-revolutionary call to arms.

It was never *not* going to be a controversial film. Perhaps unsurprisingly, the ensuing panic saw an attempt by French authorities to not only ban the film but to physically destroy all copies, and in Pennsylvania, USA, the film was described as being a training manual for potential mutineers. In the UK the film's release was a textbook example of bad timing. After the General Strike in May of the same year, which had collapsed after nine days, the freshly-elected Conservative government was fearful of another working-class rebellion and the idea of a Russia-style revolution seemed a real possibility.

Under pressure from the new Home Secretary, Sir William Joynson-Hicks, the BBFC was effectively ordered to ban the film, which, regardless of government intervention, would have still have fallen foul of its own draconian rules about showing the relation between labour and capital. The film remained banned until 1954, and even then, it was only granted an X certificate.

In the 1930s the BBFC banned a number of films for various reasons, not just political. Among them were Tod Browning's *Freaks* (1932), the Bela Lugosi and Charles Laughton vehicle *Island of Lost Souls* (1932) and a Mickey Mouse animated short called *The Mad Doctor* (1933) which was deemed 'too horrific'. But it was a film that was initially submitted for approval in 1936, and temporarily rejected by the BBFC on the grounds of it being 'a very sordid story in a very sordid surrounding', that played a small role in the way that working-class people and their ideas and lives would be portrayed in the upcoming inter- and post-war years. This film was John Baxter's *Love on the Dole* (1941).

The push for Nazi appeasement, led by many countries and governments and backed by high-profile media outlets like the BBC and many of the now-dominant Hollywood studios, was thrown into sharp relief once the Allies entered into a war with Germany in 1939. The war, as far as Britain was concerned, saw a lot of changes and hardships. Not only did the country see the introduction of government rationing and military conscription, it saw families struggling for adequate food provision and sons and fathers sent to the front line, and also many towns and cities were obliterated during the Blitzkriegian onslaught that quickly followed.

There were changes afoot for the BBFC too. Though it could already limit certain freedoms of expression or suppress them altogether, as with

Battleship Potemkin, there was a desire from the Government that under such a national emergency there should be even stricter controls on the production and release of films and footage, particularly if those films could be used as potential propaganda tools in the war effort. The Ministry of Information (MOI) was formed ostensibly to issue and vet propaganda, however it effectively took over, or at least vetoed, the decisions of the BBFC and individual councils if it believed that the film being released could hinder its fight with the Nazis.

And while this sounds as though restrictions on film-makers were getting tougher, and in some cases they were, the other effect was that many of the stricter political constraints that the BBFC had stuck rigidly to in a pre-war situation were now loosened or dropped. One of the reasons for this was that there was growing unease among poorer communities, both in the North and South, where many families who were surviving in abject poverty were still expected to accept a system which not only saw relatives being killed in battle but also kept a wealthy minority in the luxury to which it had grown accustomed.

There were reports of civil unrest and on one occasion, during a visit to a bombed area in the East End of London, the King and Queen were booed and jeered. If the war was to be won, they would need to get the working classes on side. The ban on showing the relation between capital and labour was jettisoned. According to Tom Dewe Mathews in *Censored*: 'The imperative then of the MOI was not to hinder realistic, relevant films but the exact opposite, to encourage their production. And the remarkable figure of only four films banned throughout the war implies that the MOI succeeded in the first stage of its mission to inform.'

And so, John Baxter's *Love on the Dole*, rejected twice before the war, was finally given a general UK release in 1941. In some respects, it is quite a remarkable film. In others, it very obviously isn't, but I'll discuss those later. The story, based on the 1933 novel by Walter Greenwood, and set in Hanky Park, a smoggy, Salford industrial slum, is far more hard-hitting than I had expected. The copy I viewed was a rough, slightly out of focus, internet upload, replete with a weirdly unnerving, half-heard conversation which played out beneath the actual dialogue of the film. I found myself gripped, for at least a good chunk of the action, particularly by its distinctly naked form of grim monochrome melodrama.

During the film's grinding narrative, which stumbles through narrow cobbled streets, grimy factory floors and dank and dingy parlour rooms, we witness civil unrest, industrial fatality, pre-marital pregnancy and a horde of disgruntled workers who go toe to fist with the fascist-like local constabulary. As the title suggests, we also see the soul-destroying effects of early twentieth-century unemployment in a forgotten northern town, including family break-ups, homelessness and the revolving-door hopelessness of pawn shop degradation. For the time, it was controversial stuff. There were the first hints of a style that we would later learn to call 'kitchen sink', and there are characteristics and scenes which uncannily seem to presage 60s television fare like *Coronation Street* and *Boys From the Black Stuff*. And though it is obviously an adaption of Greenwood's book there are also strong elements of Robert Tressell's much earlier Marxist tract, *The Ragged Trousered Philanthropists*, particularly when we see outspoken union man Larry attempt to educate his fellow workers about the futility of hard-line capitalism.

But the film's narrative is patchy and the characters (with the possible exception of the female parlour room quartet, who provide much-needed light relief and act as a kind of Greek chorus between other scenes) seem stiff and unlikeable. It doesn't help that two of the main male characters are called Larry and Harry. I kept forgetting who was who as their thin characterisations provided little to go on. Another problem the film has is its tendency to divide its host of working-class characters into handy stock interpretations — the proud working father, the spiv or lazy criminal type, the wanton woman or the forelock-tugging gossip. But a stumbling block for me is the desire of the filmmakers to place the misery of the situation in the foreground of every scene. This leaves little visible or emotional space for us to get to know or learn to understand why we should care about the people whose lives are being played out on screen. The story should come first and it doesn't. It plays out somewhere behind the muggy, rain-drenched poverty porn, but it spends so much of its time being beaten down by the demanding deprivation that in the end it winds up being too weak to defend itself and just gives in.

While some of *Love on the Dole*'s rudiments would be picked away at and provide the foundations for later and better films detailing the lot of working-class people, I think, on the whole, it fails as a piece of war-time cinema. To qualify that statement, I think that most British films in that period failed, at least artistically. It would take a while for the UK's film industry to grow to the point where it could even think about rivalling other more successful fare that was coming out of Europe and Hollywood.

Many Stateside directors were as acutely aware of the kind of conditions that were prevalent in *Love on the Dole*. America was also going through the Great Depression, but the key point is that they were able to produce work which encapsulated a social message, and ultimately provided much-needed entertainment and escapism for its increasingly ragged populace. And if that sounds like a sweeping, slightly unfair statement, take a movie like Frank Capra's pre-code[1] screwball comedy, *It Happened One Night* (1934). This is a charming, witty 'will-they-or-won't-they' story concerning a down-at-heel journalist (Clark Gable) and an escaping heiress (Claudette Colbert), who set out on a bickering, war-of-words road journey which leads to a blossoming romance. It's a beautifully-constructed film, well-presented and exquisitely acted and directed. And yet in spite of its Hollywood escapism, unashamed sheer entertainment value and glittering star quality, it is ultimately as critical of the uneven system as *Love on the Dole* purports to be. Look closely at the road trip the two would-be-lovers in *It Happened One Night* take, with its shabby buses, cheap boarding houses and constant references to food, or lack of food. Penny-pinched mothers and hungry children lurk on the edges of this Golden Age classic, and the rich are presented as guileless or buffoonish. Capra's blows are aimed squarely below the belt. And yet the focus is still clearly on the leading characters and it is our fascination with these people that allows us to take in the film's more important message.

Compare this with the over-long holiday sequence in *Love on the Dole*, where the film's two young lovers, fresh from a win on the horses, take a well-earned trip to the seaside. Even as the couple frequent dance halls and fairgrounds and wonder at the luxury of an indoor toilet, we are never allowed to escape their degradation. The glow of the Blackpool Illuminations cannot outshine Harry's bitterness which bubbles up throughout this boring and seemingly pointless segue.

Although the film was well-received critically, it failed to make much of a splash at the box office, and it's perhaps easy to see why audiences wouldn't have responded well, particularly those from poorer communities, given the film's dour setting and constant misery. And while there was a growing desire by the working classes to see

---

[1]   A term used to describe films which were released before the (American) Motion Picture Production Code/Hays Code was fully enforced

themselves reflected more fairly on the silver screen and in politics, what a film like *Love on the Dole* hadn't provided was larger-than-life characters and unforgettable protagonists. But by the end of the 1950s, at the start of the British New Wave, the cinema would be full of them.

3: Bombsites and Bombshells

It was the smell which had upset me most. There was nothing there
now but a faint mustiness; but on the bad morning it had been
chokingly strong — the blitz smell, damp plaster and bonemeal.
                                                    Room at the Top (1959)

By the time *Saturday Night and Sunday Morning*'s Arthur Seaton had
tumbled drunkenly down the steps of the White Horse pub in
Nottingham, his grinning rebellious face goading us into alehouse
widescreen backstreet debauchery, a different attitude was creeping
into the country. Though the 50s had only just ended, to some, that
decade was already starting to feel like a distant memory. Rock 'n' roll
saw the rise of the teenager; the Pill, introduced in 1960, waved in a
new era of sexual liberation; and for once, the largely union-supported
industries and their employees were getting a better financial deal.
These pivotal moments and societal shifts were perhaps never better
captured than on the smoke-obscured projected images of the British
silver screen. For a time, cinemas became home to a new wave of angry
young men and women. Northern- and Midlands-based anti-heroes,
wrought from the pages of Alan Sillitoe, Stan Barstow and John Braine,
stalked the packed movie houses, giving rise to a new strain of beer-
fuelled, licentious working-class swagger. Gone were the pre-war
cap-doffing characters, this was an era of uncompromising fury. But
the revolution was short-lived and for many its death knell came with
the release of the tragic Lindsay Anderson-directed feature *This
Sporting Life*. The kitchen sink presentations quickly became passé,
and the 'grim up north' mentality was in danger of deteriorating into
middle-class exploitation. As Keith Waterhouse once claimed, 'It
became impossible to move on a northern slagheap without tripping
over the film cables of a crew from the south.' But in this chapter I
want to examine the rise and popularity of those seminal films, and
to do this we need to go back to the bombed-out streets of post-war
Britain.

Despite the interference of the Ministry of Information in relation to
Love on the Dole, during the war, and immediately after it there was a
return to some of those forelock-tugging stereotypes and upstairs-
downstairs class distinctions.

David Lean and Noël Coward's production, *In Which We Serve*
(1942), is an incorrigible and not particularly interesting piece of

wartime propaganda, which now feels obsessed with class divisions. The film's sympathies lay clearly at the feet of the upper ranks. The paternal and God-like Captain, played by Coward, is suitably posh and impossibly irritating. Despite the appearance of a plucky John Mills, the working-class types are reduced to no more than barely cobbled-together stock characters, eager to throw themselves in front of a torpedo to save their establishment betters.

In the aftermath of the Second World War, not surprisingly, there was a lack of appetite for more battle-torn adventures. Families had been through enough and, in many cases, were still mourning their own very real casualties. Popular films in that period proved to be more escapist fare or pictures about larger-than-life characters. UK audiences flocked to see *The Wicked Lady* (1945), *The Bells of St Mary's* (1946), and *The Jolson Story* (1946). Other films, slightly darker in tone, like *The Seventh Veil* (1945), which depicted a suicidal mental patient, and Ealing's bizarre early British horror *The Dead of Night* (1946), also proved popular, but in general there was a need to look forward, to seek non-war-related material. There were also several attempts to depict the 'respectable' working-class family. A key example of this was the portrayal of the Huggett family in the 1947 feature *Holiday Camp*.

I have a soft spot for Ken Annakin's *Holiday Camp* but it's an odd post-war piece. Its tone sits somewhere between an episode of *Hi De Hi* and *Psycho*. The plot (or plots, as there are a number of stories playing out here in an almost portmanteau-style format) pretty much centres on the long-awaited summer vacation of an ordinary family, the Huggetts, consisting of Dad, Joe (Jack Warner), Ma, Ethel (Kathleen Harrison), widowed daughter Joan (Hazel Court), and son, Harry (Peter Hammond). Though a fairly affable bunch, they are perhaps a stale depiction of how the working classes are supposed to fit into respectable society. The camp, a sort of Butlin's, plays temporary home (or arguable microcosm) to all nature of characters and class types, and it is not so much the way the Huggetts deport themselves on holiday as how they compare in their deportment with the other campers. These include Esther (Flora Robson), the middle-class maiden aunt who is unquestionably wise, Hardwick (Dennis Price), the posh, unscrupulous squadron leader, and a host of more minor characters. Though the Huggetts are clearly where our focus lies (they would go on to star in three of their own films and a popular radio show), it's the action that occurs on the periphery of the main storyline which is more indicative of post-war class perceptions. Take Hardwick, who is revealed to be a predatory serial murderer. His actions appear to go unnoticed by society, largely because a) he is of a class which is very rarely questioned and b) his educational background (and therefore intelligence) puts him above the more easily-duped members of the lower orders. Young Elsie (Esma Cannon), for instance, who becomes one of Hardwick's victims, denotes a typically dim working-class stereotype — easily outwitted by her 'better', an upper-class wanted killer.

In the same year, Robert Hamer's *It Always Rains on Sunday* offered a more artful glimpse into the working-class community. Seemingly influenced by the romantic realism of post-war French cinema, the story, with its film noirish touches, tense set pieces and grittily realistic street scenes and interior settings, laid the groundwork for the social realism of a few decades later.

But by the 50s and the onset of the Cold War, the prospect of another international conflict became unthinkable and so a new nostalgia for the last war (which had been safely won), slowly developed on the cinema screen. The kinds of war films being made were often thinly veiled prison dramas, the action played out in the claustrophobic confines of the POW camps. These sub-genre war films such as *The Wooden Horse* (1950), though entertaining, were invariably stuffed to the gills with white upper-middle-class officers and the action usually presented itself as a boarding school romp, with the German officers being reduced to no more than not-too-bright form masters. Inevitably the working-class players were few and far between in these films, and when they appeared they were there to provide comic relief or were shoved to the side-lines as obedient yet unproductive stock characters. But the British film industry was about to receive a shock to the system.

In 1955, a little-known British film company released its own big screen version of an already-successful television sci-fi series *The Quatermass Experiment*. Retitled *The Quatermass Xperiment* to actively exploit its proudly-worn X certificate, the black and white monster movie was an instant hit. It was the first of many box office smashes for the Hammer studios. The impact of this film and the films that followed it, and its shattering of the establishment, is brilliantly communicated by David Pirie in *A New Heritage of Horror*:

> Perhaps the most astonishing thing about the film when one sees it again today is how decisively the opening

39

sequence seems to record the intrusion of Hammer into the cosy middle-class domesticity of the British Cinema. Two utterly conventional cinematic lovers run across a meadow mouthing their lines with precisely the kind of simpering coyness which had dogged British films through the 1940s and 1950s... They giggle and embrace stiffly on a convenient haystack when suddenly the whole scene is interrupted by a terrible whining noise which begins to reverberate through the darkness all around them. The noise increases to ear-shattering volume and the couple stagger to their feet and begin to run in complete disarray back across the field to take refuge in in a house. Later, when the noise has stopped, a man ventures outside and we see a huge tubular rocket-ship — which by present standards looks less like an aircraft than some surreal pronged phallus — has plunged into the ground close to where they have been lying. It would be difficult to conceive of a more symbolic or appropriate beginning for Hammer's eruption into the British film scene in the late 1950s.

Though Hammer had been around since 1936, it was in the mid-50s that it most definitely arrived in all its bloody glory, revelling in sex, seduction and exquisite thrills, quickly following *Quatermass* with its run of richly colourful horror productions. *The Curse of Frankenstein* (1957), *Dracula* (1958) and *The Mummy* (1959) were fine examples of what would become Hammer's stock in trade — beautifully-made gothic romps, replete with vampires, rugged castles, busty heroines and plenty of Kensington Gore. Brilliant British character actors like Christopher Lee and Peter Cushing regularly stalked the seemingly never-ending run of imaginative tales brought to the screen by director Terence Fisher, writer Jimmy Sangster and others. And while Hammer films were not overtly political — the studio chiefs were concerned with making money not social commentary — there is no doubt that the films were made with the working classes in mind. Hammer's approach was not only markedly different to the more antiquated and genteel films pouring out of the UK film industry, it also drove a stake through the heart of the post-war hypocrisies that still loomed on the horizon along with the crumbling city bomb sites. As Sinclair McKay points out in *A Thing of Unspeakable Horror*, when discussing Hammer's 1966 cult classic *The*

Plague of the Zombies, 'Hammer, as a rule, has no time for the ethereal half-world of bad dreams. Instead, the studio seeks to convey the impossible through a sort of brutal confrontationalism. In fact, what *Plague* represents is a studio keenly aware of the class make-up of its core audiences. For the heart of the film is not so much gothic horror as the equally pulse-quickening theme of upper-class vileness.' A quick look at the villains and ne'er-do-wells as presented in many other Hammer horror films will perhaps tell you who the intended target of most of these simple stories was — Frankenstein, for instance, may have been a twisted scientist bent on creating life, but he was also a rich baron, an unchecked and unquestioned authority, a killer run amok. There is also the Marquis in the prologue of *The Curse of the Werewolf* (1961), a sadistic tyrant who takes delight in humiliating a poor beggar who stumbles upon his wedding day celebrations. And then of course there is Dracula, a suave, hypnotic and irresistible force that stalks the shadows, unseen by most until it's too late. Has there ever been a better (if unintentional) metaphor for uncontrolled free market capitalism, a beast which sucks the life out of the innocent and offers nothing in return?

Another film franchise, which was initially as popular as Hammer and seemed to run almost in parallel to it, was the *Carry On* series. The run of films, overseen by Peter Rogers and Gerald Thomas, distributed first by Amalgamated Films and later Rank, has fallen into legend. Quite simply, they are part and parcel of our culture, as British as fish and chips or a pair of Brexit Y-fronts. Beginning with *Carry On Sergeant* in 1958, released just months after Hammer's *Curse of Frankenstein*, the series exploded, making stars of its regular list of actors which included Sid James, Kenneth Williams, Barbara Windsor and Hattie Jacques. Over the years, the films went from cheeky sea-side postcard nods and winks to out-and-out smut, deciding to up the ante on the nudity stakes in order to try and combat dwindling cinema crowds. At best, though, the *Carry Ons*, like the Hammer films, knew their core audience. Indeed, many of the first run of films centred on traditionally working-class professions as in *Carry On Cabby*, *Carry on Nurse*, and *Carry On Constable*. The middle or upper classes in these features are often presented as idiotic, eccentric or as oddly grotesque. Interestingly, *Carry On at Your Convenience* (1971), which carries a distinctly (if half-hearted) anti-union message, fared miserably at the box office. It was the franchise's first flop. While it isn't a great film and public tastes were changing in a more general sense, (its daft sexual coyness was beginning to look distinctly out-dated), it didn't help that the film seemed to be attacking its own loyal fan base.

Hammer's brand of gothic horror would give up the ghost in the late 70s, around the same time that an aging Kenneth Williams was bravely attempting to hold together what was left of the *Carry On* franchise, with the truly awful *Carry On Emmanuelle* (1978), but away from the bloodletting theatrics and comic bawdiness, back in the 50s, another entirely different set of filmmakers was beginning to make its mark.

From 1945, a Labour government had radically altered the face of a bombed-out Britain. They had ushered in the National Health Service and nationalised key industries. In general terms this had helped provide better pay, conditions and opportunities for an otherwise beleaguered workforce, who were still struggling to exist in a war-ravaged country. But by the mid-50s, the electorate had voted in another Conservative government, and while it was recognised that the effects of a post-war austerity had been elevated somewhat, as epitomised in in Macmillan's 'You've never had it so good' soundbite, there was a growing unease and a feeling that the need for actual social change had stalled somewhere along the way.

But if social change was slow in coming, a cultural shift was much quicker on its feet. In 1955, rock 'n' roll was beginning to make its presence known and a year later a poor white trash kid from Memphis would change the face of modern music forever. The teenager was born and the newly-constructed drive-in cinemas across the Atlantic capitalised on this with late-night presentations of cheaply-made independent B movies by the likes of exploitation king Roger Corman. These films not only threatened the status quo of the Hollywood monopoly but actively paid attention to its younger target audience and their newly-acquired disposable income. The film *Blackboard Jungle* with its Bill Haley *Rock Around the Clock* soundtrack caused a riot when shown at a South London picture house in the Elephant and Castle. Years of pent-up adolescent angst was unleashed in a hail of ripped-up cinema seats and crêpe-soled stomping dance moves which sent the establishment reaching for the moral panic button. Other films like Charles Laughton's *The Night of the Hunter*, starring a brutish and reverential Robert Mitchum, tapped into the darker side of a national psyche and began to pull apart the sacred cows of family and Christian piety. Nicholas Ray's *Rebel Without a Cause* captured not only the tortured confusion of arthouse heart-throb James Dean, who died just months later, but also the concerns of wider society, which was slowly being consumed by a broadening generation gap, communist scares and encroaching Cold War paranoia.

In Britain, television was becoming ever more popular. Sales of individual sets had been on the increase since the Queen's televised coronation in 1952, and the Television Act of 1954 meant that commercial companies like ITV could provide opposition to the BBC's reign. One of the most popular TV shows from that era was Nigel Kneale's *Quatermass Experiment*, and though clearly a fantasy sci-fi, it left its viewers with some unsettling imagery, none more so than when the hideous alien plant creature crawled over Westminster Abbey, threatening to destroy the world from the very building that just a year earlier had been the venue for the royal crowning. It was a stark reminder that in an age of rising East/West nuclear tension, nothing, no matter how familiar or traditional, was indestructible in the face of possible Soviet annihilation.

But away from the established companies and the rigid, production-line-style processes set in place at studios like Ealing, Bray and Elstree, a small group of experimental factual film-makers were about to unleash their highly influential dogma on the world, kick-starting the British New Wave of cinema.

Free Cinema was the loose title given to a series of six programmes of new documentaries shown at the National Film Theatre in London, which ran between 1956 and 1959. The 'Free' of the title really referred to the fact that they were made outside of the mainstream film industry and eschewed the idea of 'box office' or any kind of propaganda. But the 'movement' was never intended to be so. That the key players (including Karel Reisz, Lindsay Anderson, Tony Richardson and Lorenza Mazzetti) came together to show their films at all was largely down to pragmatic reasons — they simply couldn't find established outlets to show their work. Regardless of this, their output certainly shared a common attitude and style. The documentaries were short, invariably black and white, made with lightweight, handheld cameras, often featured no voice-overs, used non-synchronised soundtracks, and aimed their focus at largely-forgotten working-class communities. As the series note for the third programme of *Free Cinema* presentations stated, 'British cinema [is] still obstinately class-bound; still rejecting the stimulus of contemporary life, as well as the responsibility to criticise; still reflecting a metropolitan, Southern English culture which excludes the rich diversity of tradition and personality which is the whole of Britain.'

Indeed, the *Free Cinema* 'manifesto' read not so much as an informative statement but as a petulant wolf marking its territory in an already crowded environment:

> As filmmakers, we believe that
>   No film can be too personal.
>   The image speaks. Sound amplifies and comments.
>   Size is irrelevant. Perfection is not an aim.
>   An attitude means a style. A style means an attitude.

Although the movement (often dismissed as such by Lindsay Anderson) was short-lived, its body of work was impressive and still retains its status as an important entry in the history of British film production. Films like Anderson's *O Dreamland* (1953), and Reisz's *We Are the Lambeth Boys* (1959), which portrayed the day-to-day lives of a group of teenagers at a Kennington youth club, were uncompromising and raw and, even when viewed today, retain a power often absent in modern film-making. While these films were undoubtedly significant and continue to be studied and re-evaluated, it is the part they played in a wider artistic shift that was taking place in the UK which was vital. It was a shift which would, for a while at least, open up a vibrant working-class culture to a hungry cinema-going public.

4: Don't Let the Bastards Grind You Down

Mam called me barmy when I told her I fell off a gasometer for a bet. But I'm not barmy, I'm a fighting pit prop that wants a pint of beer, that's me. But if any knowing bastard says that's me I'll tell them I'm a dynamite dealer waiting to blow the factory to kingdom come. I'm me and nobody else. Whatever people say I am, that's what I'm not because they don't know a bloody thing about me! God knows what I am.

Saturday Night and Sunday Morning (1960)

For it was Saturday night, the best and bingiest glad-time of the week, one of the fifty-two holidays, in the slow turning Big Wheel of the year, a violent preamble to a prostrate Sabbath. Piled up passions were exploded on Saturday night, and the effect of a week's monotonous graft in the factory was swilled out of your system in a burst of goodwill. You followed the motto of 'be drunk and be happy', kept your crafty arms around female waists, and felt the beer going beneficially down into the elastic capacity of your guts.

When Alan Sillitoe wrote these words for his novel *Saturday Night and Sunday Morning*, the factory he was referring to was the Raleigh Factory in Nottingham, one he was familiar with as one of its ex-employees. His home county was synonymous with Robin Hood, and it had also given birth to D.H. Lawrence and homed Lord Byron, Graham Greene and even J.M. Barrie. Nottingham was a city at the heart of a heavily industrial wider county, a land of coal mines, hosiery mills, back-to-back poverty and grinding, relentless, choking toil.

Though his family was often on the brink of starvation and his own father was illiterate, Sillitoe became one of a raft of noted new writers who seemed to be bucking against the restrictive, closed-shop perspectives of the entitled bourgeois literati. Alongside other novelists and playwrights such as Stan Barstow, John Braine, Keith Waterhouse and Harold Pinter, Sillitoe was cast as one of the 'Angry Young Men', and soon the anti-heroes which populated his and other people's work would rip themselves from the printed page and provincial theatres and fight their way drunkenly onto the British silver screen.

Like Sillitoe, John Osborne was also from the Midlands, and his strongly autobiographical play *Look Back in Anger* was based in part on his unhappy marriage in a tiny bedsit in Derby. Written in just over a fortnight, it would eventually premiere, under Tony Richardson's direction, at the Royal Theatre in London. It went on to receive a host of negative reviews, but Kenneth Tynan, a hugely influential critic, championed the play describing it as a 'minor miracle'. Later, Sillitoe would say that '[Osborne] didn't contribute to British theatre, he set off a landmine and blew most of it up.'

Another admirer of the play was Canadian impresario Harry Saltzman. Saltzman was so impressed by the piece he that he persuaded Osborne and Richardson to set up a company called Woodfall Films, so that the three of them could produce and release a film adaptation.

Yet despite Saltzman's admiration of the stage play, he was initially against the idea of Richardson handling the direction duties on the celluloid version. This was understandable, for despite his *Free Cinema* offerings, Richardson was completely inexperienced when it came to mainstream film productions. It was for this reason that original backers J. Arthur Rank pulled out of the deal. Osborne was adamant that Richardson was the right person for the job and after securing Richard Burton in the lead role at a hugely reduced fee, and employing *Quatermass* writer Nigel Kneale to handle the screenplay, *Look Back in Anger* went into production and was released in 1959.

Despite excellent performances from Burton and co-star Clare Bloom, and nominations for four BAFTAs, the film failed to do well during its initial theatrical run. Its lack of success, blamed partly on some councils awarding the film an X certificate and partly on an unexpected British heatwave, could not have done much for the confidence of Richardson or Osborne, but they quickly followed this up with another Osborne play adaptation, *The Entertainer* (1960), starring Laurence Olivier. However, it was Woodfall's next three productions which would cement them into the very foundations of the British New Wave.

Woodfall's own brand of 'kitchen sink' drama seemed to be born out of not only earlier films such as *It Always Rains on Sunday* (1947) and *Love on the Dole*, and the ethos of the *Free Cinema* documentaries, but they also owed much to European productions from across the Channel. Indeed, the third *Free Cinema* programme had included the showing of work by foreign film-makers such as Roman Polanski, Claude Chabrol and François Truffaut, and their higly individual approaches to cinema undoubtedly had an influence on Richardson, Anderson, Karel Reisz and others.

In France, younger directors were making a conscious effort to shift not only from the country's recent war-time collaborations but also from the domination of the heavy literary adaptations which saturated the booming post-war market. Long tracking shots, jump cuts and hand-held cameras were employed to create a sense of ambiguity and these stylistic choices were heightened by the use of more free-flowing narratives, methods at which the mainstream studios and Hollywood would have baulked. It was the age of the 'auteur'.

Italy, like France, was attempting to shake off its political past. Under Mussolini's regime, much of the country's film output had been reduced to bland, non-transgressive productions, colourless melodramas and weak comedies featuring forgettable middle- and upper-class characters. Nicknamed 'Telefoni Bianchi' because of their lavish Art Deco sets which often featured prominent white telephones, these films disappeared at the end of the war, when not only was Mussolini destroyed, but also many of the country's film studios. This led to a more pragmatic approach, signifying cultural change and social progress. Smaller productions moved onto to the streets, using real locations and non-professional actors who starred in stories where the emphasis was switched from the privileged to the working class or down-at-heel. Children were often a focus of these neorealist productions and masterpieces like Vittorio De Sica's *Bicycle Thieves* (1948) influenced Woodfall and, later, the films of Ken Loach.

Despite the unmistakable European influence, Woodfall's films bore their own distinctive brand. Unplanned pregnancy, back-street abortions and broken marriages all played heavily in their take on modern cinema. Like the more progressive films from France and Italy, Woodfall provided an alternative. In contrast to Hollywood's silver screen, Woodfall offered a view of the world through grimy broken windows. Unlike some American productions, there was no singing but plenty of rain.

And so it was with their next film, a boozy, back-to-back melodrama of adultery, pub brawls and the factory floor. *Saturday Night and Sunday Morning* was released in 1960, and went on to be the third most popular film at the British box office that year. The newspapers may have been divided but one thing was for sure, the best anti-hero of the twentieth century had arrived and he had no more time for the critics than he had for a 'cock-eyed rent collector'.

The film was directed by Karel Reisz and produced by Tony Richardson. It was beautifully shot by Freddie Francis, who had also worked for Hammer and Amicus and who went on to produce the exquisite black and white cinematography for David Lynch's *The Elephant Man* in 1980. Like Sillitoe's novel, the film offered a matter-of-fact glimpse into an industrial working class that would no longer put up with being portrayed as a victim or something to be pitied, but more important than that, it gave us Arthur Seaton, brilliantly played by Albert Finney.

Finney, who had already appeared in Woodfall's previous film, *The Entertainer*, was a Salford-born son of a bookmaker. Graduating from the Royal Academy of Dramatic Art, he had made his London theatre debut just two years previously. Throughout his later career he moved effortlessly and convincingly from role to role, starring in films as diverse as children's musical *Annie* (1982) and the grim Coen brothers' gangster piece *Miller's Crossing* (1990). He went on to play Tom Jones, Poirot, Churchill and even Scrooge, and though he was a consummate professional actor of unique talent, to many he will always and forever be Arthur Seaton.

'Take a good look at this face,' demanded the original trailer, and so we might, as there is something about that face and the way Finney toys with the role of Seaton, as though actor and character had somehow met in the pub beforehand and thrashed out a way to work together over one (or ten) pints of bitter. His eyes sparkle furtively as he chats up Doreen (Shirley Anne Field) at the bar over a packet of crisps, but later they seem to gaze dolefully into the promise of a bleak forever when he contemplates Brenda's untimely pregnancy and possible backstreet abortion. Finney never lets up. The first time we see him as Seaton is on the Raleigh factory floor, where, via the use of a French New Wave style authorial voice-over, Seaton sets out his manifesto on modern living as he counts away his working hours using units of completed bicycle parts. 'Nine hundred and fifty-four, nine hundred and fifty bloody five,' he states over a playful Johnny Dankworth soundtrack before summing up his sermon defiantly with the immortal line: 'Don't let the bastards grind you down.' It's a tantalising screen entrance and leaves us in no doubt who is in control in this picture. Though he may suffer at the fists of the vengeful squaddies, he always comes up fighting right through to the last seconds of the film where, after being told off by Doreen for throwing a stone at a window, he promises that 'it won't be the last stone I'll throw.'

Through modern eyes, it's easy to see Seaton's many faults. He's a drunken, violent, sexist misanthrope, who thinks nothing of knocking off his mate's Mrs on the side or shooting his neighbour in the backside with an air rifle, but ultimately the reason he fascinates is because he is all about swagger, swagger and charisma.

With his brutish bar-room philosophy and immaculate hand-cut suits, Seaton is also a construct of many contradictions. Though he is in some ways the embodiment of working-class culture, he is also quick to admonish those from his own background, particularly his parents, who he insists are 'dead from the neck up'. And though he is inherently rebellious, he is ultimately apolitical. He does nothing to buck the system on a larger scale, happy instead to be king of his limited environments — the oil-soaked Raleigh factory floor and the dingy working men's club.

And while he is a non-political figure, the words that spill from his lips — 'What I want is a good time, all the rest is propaganda' — seem to take on a new meaning in a post-Brexit, Donald Trump-dominated political environment. In short, though he was torn out of the back end of 1950s, with its rationing, factories and back-to-back housing, Seaton is equally a product of today, a poster boy for twenty-first century foodbanks, zero-hour contracts and a growing mistrust of authority.

Where the film differs slightly from the book is that we are given a more ambiguous version of Seaton. While the all-important bluster is there, there are moments, particularly towards the end of the film, where we experience a less cocksure character, one who is not so much an angry young man as a confused one, recovering not only from a hangover and a beating from the soldiers, but from the realisation that the world he inhabits is changing fast and his place in it may not be so secure. This also ties in with the film's central theme of deceit. Not only does Seaton deceive his family, the women in his life and his workmates, ultimately, he also deceives himself.

But while he may be a liar and a cheat, he is also very much alive and like many a screen icon before him, this is where his appeal lies. We understand that he is likely to burn more brightly in ninety minutes than most of us will in our entire lives.

Though the film revolves around Albert Finney's excellent performance as Arthur, there is also a fantastic supporting cast, including Rachel Roberts as the married Brenda, who enters into an illicit and ill-advised affair with Seaton. There is also Shirley Anne Field who plays Doreen, who gives as good as she gets, and an early appearance by Hylda Baker, as Arthur's aunty/part time abortionist. But perhaps the real co-star is Nottingham itself, as much of *Saturday Night and Sunday Morning* was filmed on location in that very city.

Saturday Night and Sunday Morning is as entertaining as it is thought-provoking, as funny as it is tragic. It's a celluloid magic mess of melodrama, social realism, grittiness, action and ale-induced soul-searching. And the soul-searching continued in the next Woodfall production.

When we first meet Jo, the protagonist of 1961's *A Taste of Honey*, she struggles awkwardly to join in with a distinctly joyless PT class taking place in the playground of her austere-looking state school. And later, when a blonde bouffanted classmate chastises her in the changing room for her poor netball skills, Jo, without missing a beat, quips that she's 'bad on purpose'. It's in that opening line that we establish our heroine's off-kilter detachment from a system which seems designed to keep her in check. She is a natural rebel, and her intelligence and tousled unfashionable mop of hair and threadbare wardrobe mark her out to her befuddled classmates as a ragged sharp-tongued outsider. But her eyes seem alive with possibility, and there are moments, never more so than when she announces to the world that she's 'bloody marvellous', when the whole planet appears to be hers for the taking and she could easily blaze a magical trail across its endlessly fascinating landscape. But equally, those same eyes, often dark and unfathomably hollow, seem to see the world for exactly what it is. There has been no offer of a grammar school place to Jo, and despite her creativity, ingenuity and sparkle, her future will likely begin and end in the shabby world of corner-shop retail or the dingy enclosure of the factory floor. The film's location — the Salford docks — seems only to add to Jo's torment. To be trapped is one thing but to also suffer the indignity of watching an endless collection of ships bound for ocean voyages and new freedoms is another, and this helps to rack up an additional note of tragedy in this highly watchable story of mixed-race relationships, single-parent families, homosexuality and teenage pregnancy.

A Taste of Honey, the fourth Woodfall production, this time directed and co-scripted by Tony Richardson, premiered in the early autumn of 1961. Unlike Woodfall's previous film, which had turned to Sillitoe's novel as inspiration, this went back to the theatre and the work of a precocious bus inspector's daughter called Shelagh Delaney.

Like her character Jo, Delaney had been raised in Salford, Lancashire, and also like Jo, had failed her eleven plus, but her hard work and determination had seen her transferred from a nondescript secondary modern to the Pendleton High School, where she achieved five O-levels by the time she was fifteen. She wrote *A Taste of Honey*, her first play, in just ten days. 'I had strong ideas about what I wanted to see in the theatre,' she said in a 1959 interview for *Mid Century Drama*. 'We used to object to plays where the factory workers come cap in hand and call the boss "sir". Usually North Country people are shown as gormless, whereas in actual fact, they are very alive and cynical.'

The play quickly came to the attention of 'mother of modern theatre', Joan Littlewood, who developed it as part of Theatre Workshop. It premiered in Salford in 1958 and by the time Delaney was twenty it was already beginning its lengthy run of three hundred and fifty-eight performances in the West End of London. The basic story centres around seventeen-year-old Jo and her sexually promiscuous single mother Helen. When Jo is essentially abandoned by her mother, who has fallen for a young wealthy boyfriend, Peter, an uncouth and lecherous self-employed businessman, she turns at first to Jimmy, a black sailor, to whom she falls pregnant, and then to Geoff, a homosexual boy, with whom she begins sharing a flat.

With its uncompromising mix of controversial material, social issues and sharp-as-diamond dialogue, the play wore its kitchen sink credentials proudly on its sleeve, and it was only a matter of time before Woodfall came calling. The original theatrical cast had included Avis Bunnage as Helen (who would later star in film versions of *The L-Shaped Room* (1962) and *The Loneliness of the Long-Distance Runner* (1962)), Frances Cuka as Jo and Nigel Davenport as Peter. Only a young Murray Melvin, who had played Geoff on stage, would make it into the screen adaptation. Eventually, he was joined by Robert Stephens and Paul Danquah, but it's the central roles of and Jo and Helen played respectively by newcomer Rita Tushingham and future national treasure, Dora Bryan (who had already appeared in over fifty feature films since 1947) that would prove the most impressive and memorable.

The on-screen relationship between mother and daughter, brought to life via excellent performances by the two actors and the immaculate direction of Richardson, is at once hilarious, touching and unsettling. Though the constant bickering and verbal slanging matches play out within the story for the entertainment of the audience, as in the famous sequence where Geoff attempts to break up an argument between them, only to be told by Helen to 'Give over, we enjoy it', it is clear, as portrayed in quieter scenes, that Jo perhaps craves something deeper, yearns for something more solidly equated to a normal family existence.

There is a sequence in the film which features Helen and her new boyfriend Peter on a day out to Blackpool. They have taken Jo with them, much to the annoyance of Peter, who sees Jo not as potential daughter material, but as unwanted baggage. We see an unhappy Jo wander through the Hall of Mirrors, and it is here that we perhaps begin to see through Jo's eyes how her life (as represented by the misshapen reflections) has become unrecognisable, as though she is searching in vain for something she can at least pretend is an actual mother/daughter relationship. When she is finally jettisoned by her mother and Peter and forced to catch the bus home alone, it is the look in those eyes, awash with anger and heartbreak, that betrays her real feelings, feelings which go deeper than all the surface knife-edge wit and cynicism. It is as though she is admonishing herself for even believing that such feelings might exist. As she states in the film, 'I 'ate love.'

Dora Bryan, in later interviews, would often be dismissive of *A Taste of Honey*. To her it was only one of a raft of screen appearances in a career that lasted almost seventy years, but there is no doubt that her portrayal of Helen is one of the most memorable screen performances, certainly within the ranks of the kitchen sink-style presentations, but possibly one of the best that British cinema has ever seen. Previously she had played many comic roles including the dippy, love-struck simpleton Norah in the inaugural *Carry On* feature, *Carry On Sergeant*, and while Helen often appears to the audience as a 'comic turn', particularly on her initial date with Peter when she giddily takes to the night club dance-floor displaying all the sophisticated restraint of a makeup-wearing cat on heat, there is also a frailness to the character. Her rounded performance takes the character of Helen away from simplistic 'lapsed mother' territory and into something far more complicated, making it more difficult for audience members to make moral judgements.

Perhaps she does 'abandon' her daughter but, arguably, it is because she understands that Jo is capable of achieving far more than she ever could if left to her own devices. By the end of the film it is not Jo who seeks out her wayward mother but rather Helen who seeks out Jo. For all her youthful exuberance, Jo is forced to be the adult in this situation, fearing that there will always perhaps be something inadequate about Helen. Ultimately Jo understands that her mother is no more than a child, who when faced with an opportunity to escape, took it, failed and came crawling back.

Her mother's absence means that Jo, at first embroiled in a romantic liaison with Jimmy, a black sailor who goes back to sea, eventually shacks up with Geoff, a gay man who has recently been chucked out of his digs for reasons undisclosed. It is this relationship, which plays out largely in the confines of their dingy attic space, or against the backdrop of a post-war Salford replete with its clogged canals and back-to-back housing, that is perhaps the most endearing. Geoff becomes not only Jo's friend but also her surrogate brother and housekeeper, and when he learns of Jo's pregnancy, even considers becoming her stand-in husband.

Murray Melvin, who plays Geoff, is a revelation in this pivotal role, right from his first appearance, when he trails skulkily after Jo, hoping that he's at last stumbled upon a fellow outsider with whom he can share his world, to the fabulously awkward scene where an incredulous midwife hands him family planning advice and a strange-looking practice doll, so that he might best support his friend's upcoming maternity. There is, for a while at least, an unshakeable strength in Geoff, a steadfastness which presents itself more clearly during Jo's darker moments, like when she admonishes Geoff for bringing home a maternity doll that's 'the wrong colour' or when she sinks into despair, fearing that her unborn child might turn out to be 'simple'.

Delaney and Richardson's script coupled with Murray's excellent turn as Geoff, present us with, for the most part, a startlingly different portrayal of young male homosexuality, shunned by other British and American productions. The Sexual Offences Act, which ushered in the decriminalisation of sexual relationships between male adults, would not come into place till 1967. Until then such 'practices' were illegal and could be punished by lengthy prison sentences or barbaric methods of chemical castration. Such restrictions both here and in the US meant screen portrayals of male homosexuals were often reduced to throwaway stereotypes, as in the 20s/30s 'cissy' characterisations of various Hollywood productions, or the representations of gay men as predators, deviants, targets or the endlessly tortured. Geoff, in the hands of Melvin, is a thoroughly rounded personality, a million miles away from the stock cinematic personifications of the past. And yet while the character is infinitely watchable — one of the key reasons we can still enjoy this beautiful film — it is in his final heart-breaking on-screen moment, where we see him wander away for good into the bonfire-flickering, darkening streets, that we understand that no matter how ground-breaking a film like *A Taste of Honey* was, wider society was still not ready for the likes of Geoff, who was cast cruelly to the edges of normality.

A Taste of Honey, both the play and the film, stand as testament to the talents of Delaney. She wrote the play when she was just eighteen and, even now, the subjects the text deals with can still raise the hackles of the right-wing press, but it is her brilliant use of dialogue and her absolute understanding of the people she is writing about which is most impressive. Shelagh Delaney died in 2011, leaving behind an unquestionable influence and legacy, which I will explore further later on in this book. For now we will move on to explore the next Woodfall production, one that would see them plundering again the works of Nottingham-born Alan Sillitoe.

> As soon as I got to Borstal they made me a long-distance cross country runner. I suppose they thought I was just the build for it because I was long and skinny for my age (and still am) and in any case I didn't mind it much, to tell you the truth, because running had always been made much of in our family, especially running away from the police…

And so begins the opening story in a collection of Sillitoe's stories released in 1959. The book contains some of the very best of Sillitoe's early material and many of the intricately created selections played out effectively in his often-overlooked East Midlands home city. In one story, *On a Saturday Afternoon*, Sillitoe deftly demonstrates not only his skilful approach to prose but also his pinpoint use of morbid comedy, as in this darkly humorous passage:

> I once saw a bloke try to kill himself. I'll never forget the day because I was sitting in the house one Saturday afternoon, feeling black and fed-up because everybody in the family had gone to the pictures, except me who'd for some reason been left out of it. 'Course, I didn't know then that I would soon see something you can never see in the same way on the pictures, a real bloke stringing himself up. I was only a kid at the time, so you can imagine how much I enjoyed it.

But it was the title story of the collection, with its anarchic anti-hero Colin Smith, that formed the basis of Woodfall's next film.

The Loneliness of the Long Distance Runner (1962) was directed again by Tony Richardson, while Sillitoe himself, as in *Saturday Night and Sunday Morning*, had been brought in to handle the screenwriting. The production also employed the cinematography of Walter Lassally, who had so beautifully rendered the on-location Salford street scenes and monochrome malaise of *A Taste of Honey*. And just as the film's text perfectly illustrated societal separations in class and the widening generation gap, the casting of the two lead roles did so also.

Born in Bristol in 1908 and son of silent screen actor Roy Redgrave (whom he never knew), Michael Redgrave was schooled at Cambridge, where his love of the theatre developed. By the end of the 1930s he was a well-established Shakespearean actor who had also made his mark on the silver screen, notably in Hitchcock's pre-war thriller *The Lady Vanishes* (1938). By the time he was cast as *The Loneliness of the Long Distance Runner*'s bloody-minded Borstal governor, Redgrave was in his mid-fifties, and as far as other thespians were concerned, he was theatrical royalty, a well-placed member of the reliable old guard.

Tom Courtenay was born in East Riding, Yorkshire, the son of a boat painter. He attended Kingston High School before gaining a place at the Royal Academy of Dramatic Art (RADA). He made his debut with the Old Vic theatre company in 1960 and later took over the title role in *Billy Liar*, (a role which he went on to play on-screen), from a young Albert Finney. If Redgrave represented the old order, then Courtenay was almost certainly an upstart newcomer.

Though there is no evidence to suggest that Courtenay and Redgrave didn't get on, from a filmmaker's point of view, it would have felt like a tantalising clash of cultures. The North/South divide, the class distinctions and the clash of older and newer ways of being were all there, writ large upon the screen before a single line of script had been spoken.

The story concerns Colin Smith (Courtenay), a scruffy, yet sharp-witted adolescent, who at not even twenty finds himself on the very bottom of an elitist system. After watching his father die a lingering death brought on by industrial negligence, Smith, who is at odds with his younger siblings and seemingly heartless mother (Avis Bunnage), turns to petty crime and thievery. His world is one of damp-looking prefabs and baked-bean teas. Rare moments of adventure are snatched, never given. Happiness comes in a random trip to out-of-season Skegness, where virginities and fortunes are lost in the wind-blown autumn dunes and the haunting shelter of the amusement arcades. After the opportunist robbery of a bakery with his equally down-at-heel partner in crime Mike (an early screen appearance of *Likely Lad* James Bolam) Smith is arrested and sent to Borstal.

The delivery of the narrative, a refreshingly creative one that employs a non-linear approach, is littered with sequences that send us back and forth through time and provide us with an uneasy build of tension.

In one memorable sequence, when Smith's mum has received the insurance money for her recently-deceased husband, she takes the family out for a 'spend up', much to her eldest son's disapproval. The whole scene plays out like some gaudy commercial, the montage is adorned with advertisements and shop signs and excited children. One of the main purchases is a new television. It plays a central role in a later scene when Mike and Colin, frustrated by their lack of options, turn the sound down on a political broadcast, providing their own commentary. It's a comic moment, but also hints at their desperate need to take control of a future that has already been decided for them.

Television was a target for many British filmmakers of the time, who were distrustful of its more commercial, less artistic attributes. This is illustrated best in *Saturday Night and Sunday Morning* by Arthur Seaton, who rails against his 'dead from the neck up' father, lost to his nightly binge of beamed-in entertainment froth.

If Seaton comes across as angry and charismatic, his personal form of rebellion only stretches as far as the factory gates or the ale-house door. With Colin Smith we get the real deal. In an early scene, Smith is grilled by Brown (Alec McCowen), a clueless middle-class counsellor, on his induction into the stark Borstal surroundings. And though he is a prisoner, Smith catches on quickly that the counsellor is as trapped as he is, no more than an aspirational, do-gooding public servant, caught forever in the nowhere world between 'low-life' Borstal inmates and unreachable upper-class management. Smith, recognising the hopelessness of the situation, turns the interview into a time-wasting game of 'us and them'.

Daily life is hard in the new regime, and gets harder when Smith is targeted by Ruxton's 'daddy' inmate after delivering a blistering attack on the system: 'Do you know what I'd do if I had the whip hand? I'd get all the coppers, governors, army officers and Members of Parliament and I'd stick 'em up against this wall and let 'em have it. 'Cos that's what they'd like to do to blokes like us.'

It is only when Smith's talent for long distance running is spotted by the governor (Redgrave), that his incarceration becomes a good deal more bearable. His role in a fight goes unpunished, much to the grievance of his bleeding opponent, and he is taken out of the soul-destroying factory and given a cushier garden job. He is even allowed to run free, unsupervised outside the Borstal's gates, such is the governor's desire to win a much sought-after school trophy.

It is perhaps in these scenes that we get the clearest underlining of the film's 'us and them' themes of class inequality. Smith may seem to enjoy his new freedoms, yet his privileges fall into stark relief when juxtaposed against the conditions that less-fortunate inmates are forced to endure. Managing to avoid the beatings, cruel working conditions and bread and water rations, Smith appears to have learned how to play the system for his own benefit, much in the way that Seaton had in *Saturday Night and Sunday Morning.*

Later, he is reunited with Mike, who has ended up in the same Borstal, and his friend seems perturbed by Smith's level of cooperation and subservience. He chastises his unrecognisable old companion and we, the audience, also begin to wonder whether Smith has finally been co-opted.

There are more scenes of class distinctions and power imbalances such as the famous 'Jerusalem' segment and when we first meet the rival running team, an unmistakably privileged bunch of private school toffs who mix uneasily with the 'scruffy criminal Herberts'.

It is only in the last moments of the film when we see Smith deliver his master stroke, as he throws away his chance to be the victor in an easily winnable race, an act which sends the establishment (as represented by Redgrave's governor) into fits of red-faced disbelief, that we understand what the game has been all along. His final defiance is just that, a selfless act of random disobedience. And unlike Seaton, whose own petty swipes at the establishment only seem to hurt those around him, such as pregnant Brenda or her broken-hearted husband, it is Smith and Smith alone who pays the price for his scurrilous sedition. Stripped again of his privileges and cast back into the dingy factory, with its beatings, humiliations and bread and water conditions, Smith has made the ultimate sacrifice.

There is a bleakness to *The Loneliness of the Long Distance Runner.* Even its seaside scenes are presented as cold and desolate. Silhouettes haunt a deserted beach like ghostly atmospheric stills from a long-lost film noir, but there is a sharpness too. Like its two predecessors the dialogue is whip-smart, funny and at times furious, often all three, as in this early exchange between Smith and the governor and his lackey.

> The Governor: And yours? [meaning his name]
> Smith: Smith
> Lackey: Say sir when you answer the governor
> Smith: Sir Smith

The film, an undoubted classic, acts as a grim template for later work like *Scum* (1979), *Made in Britain* (1982) and even *Quadrophenia* (1979), but its legacy can be felt in television and various other forms of literature. It would be hard to imagine shows like *This is England '86*, or Irvine Welsh's *Trainspotting*, without the influence of Sillitoe's light-footed protagonist. Colin Smith remains a true working-class hero and, unlike Seaton, his lasting appeal is unhampered by the latter's outdated misogyny and brutish egotism.

Woodfall Productions continued to make films until 1984, amongst them *Tom Jones* (1963), *The Charge of the Light Brigade* (1968) and *Hamlet* (1969), and they even made a return to their kitchen sink beginnings when Tony Richardson stepped in to rescue a financially problematic independent film called *Kes*, but it is perhaps their first run of films that will earn them a place in the story of working-class cinema.

5: The Other Side of the Kitchen Sink

If you're in any more trouble, Billy, it's not something you can leave behind you, you know. You put it in your suitcase, and you take it with you.

Billy Liar (1963)

While Woodfall Productions, for a time at least, seemed like the all-conquering purveyor of the cutting-edge UK scene, with their custom-made gritty kitchen sink dramas of Northern and Midlands' angry young men and women, they were not the only game in town. Other studios and filmmakers had also sensed the public's appetite for the current raft of working-class stories on the stage and bookstands.

Arguably, the first official British New Wave film was not a Woodfall production but a Romulus Films release. Romulus, headed by brothers John and James Woolf, acquired the rights to *Room at the Top*, a gutsy yet poetic novel written by John Braine in the late 50s. The book tells the story of Joe Lampton, an ambitious office worker from a poor background who ruthlessly weaves his way into the unfamiliar world of inherited wealth, middle-class social settings and adulterous betrayals. It's a beautifully written book; the masterly use of first person prose, told from the point of view of the sharp-tongued protagonist Lampton, is both entertaining and seething:

> The ownership of the Aston-Martin automatically placed the young man in a social class far above mine; but that ownership was simply a question of money. The girl, with her even suntan and her fair hair cut short in a style too simple to be anything else but expensive, was as far beyond my reach as the car. But her ownership, too, was simply a question of money, of the price of the diamond ring on her left hand. This seems all too obvious; but it was the kind of truth which until that moment I'd only grasped theoretically.

When it came to the film version (released in 1959), James Woolf approached Jack Clayton to direct. Woolf had been impressed by Clayton's earlier Academy Award-winning short *The Bespoke Overcoat*, a strange adaptation of a play that skilfully blended *Love on the Dole* grittiness with supernatural overtones. Woolf intended to cast Stewart Granger as Lampton, and was also keen to offer parts to Vivien Leigh and Jean Simmons. Eventually Laurence Harvey took on the role of Lampton with Simone Signoret as Alice and Heather Sears as Susan.

From the outset it is clear that Joe Lampton is no Arthur Seaton, and that's probably the point. Harvey's portrayal of the character is a wildly different beast from Sillitoe's anti-hero. When he moves from his home town of Dufton, a cheerless bombsite of back-to-backs and cobbled streets, to the (by comparison) up-and-coming Warnley, to assume his enviable post in the Treasury department, it appears that Joe's sights are set purely on the future. When his promotional prospects are laid before him by a work colleague, '…a thousand a year, a semi-detached down town, a second-hand Austin and a wife to match if you know what I mean?' Joe responds, 'I know damn well what you mean and that's why I'm going to have the lot.'

His lodgings, quite literally a room at the top, provide a handy metaphor for his unfaltering ambition, but it is not Joe's ability to look forward which betrays his character so much as his inability to forget the past. Despite Joe's progression into a world of which he so clearly craves to be part, the chip on his shoulder only grows bigger.

There is something addictively watchable yet deeply unlikeable about Lampton in the hands of Harvey. His spirit is marred by an unrelenting bitterness and his loathing for not just those silver spooners — 'They've got just about everything, haven't they?' — but also for the dutiful 'zombies' who belong to his own social class, is barely kept in check. It is his own self-imposed exile between the two groups which renders him a fascinating, though frustrating, protagonist. In a scene in which he returns to Dufton, we see Lampton, in his office attire, trampling through the wreckage of his old bombed house. Visually, it's an interesting shot, providing us with an immediate insight into the no-man's land of Joe's existence, neither ready for the middle-class life, nor willing to accept that he may still have a footing in his humble beginnings. Lampton's sense of misplace perhaps mirrors the actor's own upbringing — he was born in Lithuania and raised in South Africa, before establishing himself as an English actor.

When Joe's advances towards Susan, the daughter of rich industrialist Brown, are spurned when she is sent abroad, his working-class sensibilities bristle at the injustice of their contemptuous entitlement. Harvey excels in these moments, the character's fragility only becoming more evident at the boiling point of his rage. Like *Saturday Night and Sunday Morning*, *Room at the Top* is salacious, sexy and poignant.

Lampton's rejection by the Browns leads to a heated affair with Alice, a liaison which is wracked by guilt and post-war yearning, an erotically-charged locomotive on a collision course with harsh reality. Signoret, as Alice, is wonderfully complicated, smouldering, sullen, lost and playful. She oozes Hollywood charisma in a concrete, monochrome sordid suburbia.

The plot steers the three players in the disastrous love triangle to a tragic denouement. When Joe breaks up with Alice, to avoid public ruination at the hands of her brutish husband, she takes the split hard and dies in a drunken automobile wreck. It is with this knowledge that Lampton is forced to share a wedding car with a veiled and pregnant Susan, whose innocence is matched only by her groom's dead-eyed singularity. The indignity of their situation is understated. When tears well up in his eyes, Susan mistakes this for nuptial joy. 'I believe you really are sentimental after all,' she coos, and although Joe tries desperately to please with the most pathetic of smiles, we know that their journey together is as doomed as Alice's inebriated car ride, and never have the words THE END, central and white, felt so fitting at the climax of a film.

Jack Clayton's film is perhaps less memorable than Reisz's *Saturday Night and Sunday Morning*, as its anti-hero lacks the charisma of Seaton and Harvey is no Albert Finney. But it is a worthy film and sits comfortably within the history of working-class cinema.

Shot partly at Shepperton Studios but mostly on location in Halifax and Bradford, as with *Saturday Night and Sunday Morning*, Freddie Francis provided the crisp black and white photography, aiding and abetting the narrative's darker twists and turns. Its stark and often cynical view of modern relationships, especially the hypocrisies linked to the institution of marriage, hierarchy, status and 'the need to do the right thing' whether or not it leaves anyone happy at the end, is mercilessly explored in the sharp storyline.

In his later 1969 film, *Midnight Cowboy*, director John Schlesinger played with the idea of misfits coming together against the backdrop of New York City, a place of magical promise that somehow always eluded the tragic protagonist double act of John Voight and Dustin Hoffman. It was at times a stark and unrelentingly grim story, yet one which was dotted with moments of hope, love and camaraderie, but it was an end-of-the-decade film, one almost certainly darkened by the looming shadow of 1970. The summer of love was a long way away, the peace signs now broken fingers trapped in the closing door of Nixon's political office.

But the idea of two unsuitable people coming together and finding a way to make the best of it (or worst of it) was one that Schlesinger had already explored in his first feature, *A Kind of Loving* (1962).

The film, an Anglo Amalgamated production, was based on the 1960 novel of the same name by Yorkshireman Stan Barstow, the first of a trilogy of books that centred around Vic Brown.

> ... that was the day I decided to do something about Ingrid Rothwell besides gawp at her like a love-sick cow or something whenever she came in sight. I'd been doing this for about a month before Christmas, I remember. I don't know what started it. Does anybody know what starts these things, why a bint can be one among dozens about the place one day and somebody special the next?

Brown, perhaps initially drawn as a partly autobiographical creation, given Barstow's own working-class beginnings, grammar school education and early life as a draughtsman, becomes, in the hands of screenwriters Keith Waterhouse and Willis Hall and director Schlesinger, a much more cinematically complicated character.

Alan Bates, who took on the role, had already established himself as belonging to the first wave of kitchen sink style productions, first in the stage play of *Look Back in Anger*, later in the Woodfall film *The Entertainer* alongside his contemporary, Albert Finney, and also in the beautifully realised *Whistle Down the Wind*. But with Vic Brown, Bates presented us with another classic, if conflicted, portrayal of the angry young man.

Already wearied with the draughtsman's job he is constantly told that he should be grateful for, Vic, an affable yet slightly deeper thinker than the work friends by which he finds himself surrounded, is seeking more from life than the nine-to-five and eventual promise of a pension. 'Well, you can have a bit too much security, can't you?' he goads a boastful ex-colleague. 'I'd like to get out of this town, go somewhere else, have a look around, enjoy myself.'

It is his pursuit of more lustful pleasures that sends Vic's aspirations crashing down in a sea of societal expectation when Ingrid (June Ritchie), his none-too-serious girlfriend, falls pregnant. In a scene directly before he finds out about Ingrid's condition, Vic tragically relays his slightly confused feelings about his potential lover, making what's to come seem all the more depressing. 'Do you know, it's a funny thing, sometimes I really fancy her, the next day I can hardly stand the sight of her.'

Both trapped by what's expected of them in terms of community and family, the story descends into the desperate hours of Vic's loss of control. Forced to share a house with the raging ball of conservatism that is Ingrid's mother, Mrs Rothwell, brilliantly played by Thora Hird, who quickly pulls the trigger on their shotgun wedding, their marriage soon crumbles into a resentful arrangement of barely-concealed annoyances. And though it is Vic who is central here, it is perhaps Ingrid that we feel more sympathy for. While Vic is hampered by society's contradictions and hypocrisies it is Ingrid who will be truly trapped by them, confined not only by her working-class limitations but also by late 50s/early 60s gender restrictions.

Though Vic might desire an escape and alternative future, there are also moments in the film which betray his nostalgia for his class and background. His comfort with the 'old world', illustrated by scenes where he is cast against the remains of back-to-backs and ancient-looking factories, falls into sharp relief when juxtaposed with Ingrid's mother's cloying aspirations to join the middle classes, with her new-build house on the posh estate.

In another scene, which also skilfully depicts class distinction and the differences between the old and new worlds, we see Vic's father playing in a brass band. The camera pans across the audience and we notice that there are three empty seats. We then cut back to the living room of Mrs Rothwell, where we realise that the empty seats were meant for her, Ingrid and Vic. The three huddle around a new-fangled television set and while Ingrid and her mother seem happily engaged in the petty offerings of the small screen, Vic seems bored and dejected.

The bitterness is ramped up further when Ingrid suffers a miscarriage. The couple's sadness (at least Vic's) is not born out of the loss of a child which neither of them wanted, but more out of the irony of their situation. The problem which has trapped them is now a problem no more, yet they are still trapped. The miscarriage occurs after Ingrid falls down stairs and is hospitalised, and what makes things worse is that Mrs Rothwell deliberately fails to inform Vic. Her disapproval of the marriage is apparent from the start, but from here on in the tension builds. An already-dissatisfied Vic is driven to debauched desperation.

After returning home drunk he engages in a bitter argument with a seething Mrs Rothwell, then throws up on the carpet, causing her to unleash her barely concealed hatred. 'You pig,' she spits. It's an incendiary performance from Thora Hird. This is not the comedy mother-in-law of a Les Dawson routine, there is something much deeper to be examined and ironically that depth seems to come out of the character's utterly banal and vacuous viewpoint. Her descent into smarmy middle-class aspiration, a social group she probably knows she will never sit comfortably with, provides a handy shadow to Vic's pointless attempts to stay linked to the old world and his previous lifestyle of dancehalls, girls and cheap, tattered porno books.

His final ejection from the past seems to come when his attempted family homecoming, after leaving Ingrid, is thwarted by parents who send him packing, back to the marriage he never truly wanted.

It is only in the final moments of enforced reconciliation that Ingrid and Vic understand that while deeper passions for each other may elude them, they can at least settle for 'a kind of loving'.

The team of Schlesinger, Waterhouse and Hall reunited for another kitchen sink-style production — *Billy Liar* (1963). Much more comic in tone, the film offers us an insight into the fantasist mind of William Fisher, played by Tom Courtenay, fresh from his critical success in Woodall's *The Loneliness of the Long Distance Runner*.

Adapted from the novel of the same name, also written by Waterhouse, *Billy Liar* initially became a highly successful West End play starring Albert Finney. Courtenay understudied Finney during this run and, though Finney received excellent notices, it's difficult now, in the light of Courtenay's revelatory performance in the film, to imagine anyone else in the role.

Fisher is hardly the angry young man as presented in earlier films like *Saturday Night and Sunday Morning* or *Look Back in Anger*, and he feels a million miles away from the hate-fuelled boozy testosterone of *This Sporting Life*'s Frank. Instead, we are presented with a light-fingered, yet highly intelligent and deeply frustrated office clerk, whose escape from the mundanity of Northern industrial grind is found not in the boozers and dancehalls as presented in Sillitoe or Barstow's works, but in the playful imagination of his adolescent brain. Ambrosia, Fisher's imaginary country, where he pictures himself as military hero and demigod, in an effort to block out the realities of his complicated life, is brilliantly realised in the film. The celebratory parades and fantasy sequences featuring a bevy of appreciative dolly birds and a grinning Courtenay at his playful best provide a fitting contrast to the drab streets of Bradford and the dullness of the nine-to-five.

Fisher has much to escape from, not only the confines of restrictive job prospects (he has aspirations to become a screenwriter), but also the many, mainly self-created, difficulties which constantly bubble to the surface. Billy happens to be engaged to two different girls at the same time, and he also seems unable to cease making up stories — false rumours about his father's lost leg for instance, provide just one hilarious example of his ridiculous sense of random rebellion. There is also the small matter of workplace embezzlement — Fisher has neglected to mail out a consignment of calendars and has pocketed the postage money.

It is only when he meets Liz, played brilliantly by Julie Christie, that Billy begins to consider a more physical escape. Liz, a free-spirited eager traveller, immediately understands Fisher and can see potential where he perhaps cannot. She is the antithesis to the small-mindedness of Billy's home town. She looks different, her modern clothes and slightly unkempt hair jars with the fifties throwback local dancehall girls with their immaculate bouffant dos and standard-issue seamed nylons. She provides an alternative kind of rebellion, something much scarier than, say, Seaton's futile nihilism, because she represents the future. A future which is coming thick and fast whether Bradford wants it or not. She oozes confidence and sees the world as a playground, while Billy's contemporaries see only barriers and factory gates.

In one late-night scene, Liz and Billy talk openly about their hopes and aspirations. Liz discusses her ambitions to '… be invisible, I'd like to be able to move around without having to explain anything.' It's at this point that Billy tells her about Ambrosia, and also manages to weave in a not-so-subtle marriage proposal. '… if we were married we could just sit and imagine ourselves there.' But while Liz symbolises a more open-minded response to life and its possibilities, Billy's workmates, who, unbeknownst to the pair, lurk in the bushes behind them, certainly represent the sort of cloying small-world cynicism that pervades post-war Britain. They taunt Billy and castigate his free use of imagination and (ironically) honesty, unable to grasp his refusal to be melted into their cast-iron realities.

Liz persuades Billy to leave his home town and go with her to London and it is in the final scenes at the station that the tragedy of sorts plays out. Moments away from embarking on the adventure that he has always purported to have wanted, Billy falters at the last. Perhaps drawn back by the potential legal consequences of leaving behind his unresolved work-place thievery, or the news that his grandmother has been taken ill, Billy makes the excuse of buying milk for the journey from a nearby vending machine. He makes sure he takes his time, enough time for the train to pull away without him. We see a regretful Liz at the window disappearing out of his life in a chugging puff of locomotive diesel. On his long walk home Billy imagines himself again as the hero, leading a parade through his made-up land of Ambrosia, and though there is a smile across his face, it only helps to highlight the inner sadness of the character.

Despite the melancholy closing, in general the film leaves us feeling entertained. Billy, in Courtenay's hands, is entirely charming, charismatic, awkward yet sharp. It's an incredibly funny film, many laugh-out-loud moments are born out of the main character's inability to keep track of his own fabrications. Much humour is drawn from the fact that many characters Billy interacts with completely fail to see that he is making fun of them, his teasing is so underplayed, so expertly carried out that we cannot help but enjoy the joke, even when his own joke seems to consume him at the end of the film. But if it's humour that keeps this film alive, the same cannot be said for the next film we'll look at, a film which arguably rang the death knell for the short-lived British New Wave.

6: All the Rest Is Propaganda...

It's only a game, old sport. It's all a game.

This Sporting Life (1963)

A dark screen with stark white opening credits which appear unapologetically over a brooding, funeral death dirge. This soon transposes into the noise of a roaring crowd, which could easily be interpreted as either a celebratory union demonstration or a baying mob. This fades slowly into a quieter yet still mournful score, a chilling trickle of notes that seem to ask questions but provide no answers. Then we are dropped into the action — a brutalised depiction of a rugby league match. Frank, played by Richard Harris, at his young, physical peak, a dominating screen presence, stomps across the pitch, which is no more than a chewed up muddy field, less sports venue, more no man's land during the Battle of the Somme. He wears the number 13 shirt, a none-too-subtle hint that things aren't going to go well for him. Within moments our protagonist has his face smashed in. The monochrome production only adds to the violent tone. Frank's blood bubbles black and horrible between his broken and now useless teeth. So starts the 1963 Lindsay Anderson film version of *This Sporting Life*.

The violence portrayed on screen apparently spilled into reality during the production of this strange, humourless masterpiece. The director and his often-troubled star would occasionally come to blows. Anderson related his feelings on this in his autobiographical *The Diaries*:

> Much of the violence of [*This*] *Sporting Life* was connected with [Harris] getting his own way; and too obscured by that motivation to strike me as 'sadistic'... the punching... How or when that started I can't well remember: it may have been me that encouraged it — or in response to a threatened raised fist of his. Anyway, by the end of the picture, the bruises were marked; and sometimes the interchanges of blows quite painful. Certainly undignified. I remember one of the last shots — an insert of Richard lying on the doss house bed — and how we got involved, like two school boys, in a suddenly quite violent interchange of blows (and I with my front tooth embarrassingly loose).

And the pain didn't end there. It continued, at least in a metaphorical sense, with the film's release and its subsequent poor box office and reception. The problem was, Britain was changing again. England, particularly London, was becoming the focus of the world, not only in fashion and music but in film too. *Dr. No* (1962), the first proper James Bond feature, had been a smash, and while *Saturday Night and Sunday Morning*, for example, had been perfectly placed on the timescale of the early sixties, by the time *This Sporting Life* was released, there was an eagerness to move away from the austere and toward the more frivolous elements of that 'swinging' decade. The film's unrelentingly brutal tone sat uncomfortably with the all-too-cheery Beatles tunes that rode the waves of the burgeoning new pop scene.

But while the film was and still is an uncomfortable watch, and seems to distance itself from other kitchen sink productions (it's difficult to imagine Billy Fisher existing in the same universe as Frank Machin, for instance), it is also a cinematic gem.

People new to this film should be warned that there is no fun to be had. In other dramas of this era, the humour is evident, even if we have to wipe away at the grime to find it, but *This Sporting Life* provides no such light relief. It's a dark and at times wilfully depressing story but all the better for it.

Its non-linear, cut-up style of storytelling, with switches in time and clever use of visual set-ups, creates an awkward, yet rewarding viewing experience. More artful perhaps than its predecessors, and definitely more experimental, the strange employment of unusual narrative construction seems to foreshadow Anderson's later films like *If...* (1968) and *O Lucky Man* (1973). Based on a novel of the same name, this time by David Storey, *This Sporting Life* focuses on the none-too-likeable character of Frank Machin.

Machin (Richard Harris) is a miner and aspiring professional rugby league player. The two aspects of his life segue brilliantly in an opening sequence. First, we see Frank at the pit. A heavy industrial drill in his hands, dirt-streaked, he toils away in the near dark, grinding away at the unrelenting coalface. Then we cut away to Frank at the dentist's, after the unfortunate sporting accident. The gleaming white surroundings and tiny surgeon's instruments jar perfectly, exposing Frank's inability to sit comfortably within the high life he claims to desire. Perks like the rugby club paying for private dental care and access to the more elite nightclubs are all very well, but Machin is a natural misfit and no amount of fivers stuffed in his newly-pressed trousers will ever change that. Which is not to say that he is without ambition, but the film never lets us forget that it's an ambition for which he must pay dearly.

He is also angrier than most angry young men. It's an existential angst, perhaps more in keeping with *On The Waterfront* than *Room at the Top*. It is his own lack of understanding of the world and just exactly what his place in it is to be, that perhaps drives him into the lodgings of Mrs Hammond. Hammond, played by Rachel Roberts, is equally at odds with the world. A widower with two young children, she exists as a kind of ghost haunting the meagre house she keeps, a bitter shadow, shunning the living, her late husband's work boots kept polished by the fire. She is the quiet seething antithesis to Frank's wild outbursts, a dead-eyed phantom seeking release, the choking smoke to Frank's blazing inferno.

Their inevitable 'romance' is as rough as the sport by which Frank earns his living. Rugby League is an excellent metaphor for their unhealthy relationship — a violent battle, with, as David Rollinson points out 'brief moments of contact and fending off.'

The basic story sees Frank, a talented, if unpredictably aggressive player, recruited by his local rugby league club. He negotiates the highest sum the club has ever paid, the club recognising that his brutality might be to their advantage. Though his methods work perfectly well on the pitch, he has a tendency to try and employ the same techniques in his personal life, with much less success. The fact that he cannot barge his way through life's problems as with an opponent's scrum half, is a frustrating lesson Frank never seems to learn. Though arguably full of life himself, he is just as awkward with the living as Mrs Hammond. His team-mates distrust him and perhaps rightfully so, as there seem to be no loyalties which he won't consider breaking if it serves his own ambition. 'Dad', played by William Hartnell, is one of the first of his victims. Dad has been an open supporter of Frank's and even smooths the path for him being considered by the big leagues but, ultimately, he is jettisoned and forgotten as soon as Frank gets what he wants.

The relationship between Frank and Margaret Hammond is also doomed. It comes to an end at a team-mate's wedding which, because of Mrs Hammond's dark apparel and lingering outdoor shots of gravestones, often resembles a funeral.

Unlike other British New Wave productions, which skilfully blend pathos with humour, as in *Billy Liar* or *A Taste of Honey*, the tone of *This*

Sporting Life never budges from its unmistakable misery, so its bleak closing scenes portraying a broken Frank Machin, wandering mournfully around the empty lodging house, tearfully whispering his ex-lover's name, really come as no surprise.

Though initially praised by many critics, it was little more than a disaster at the box office. Rank, the distributors, had been bitten badly and vowed never to have anything to do with kitchen sink drama again. The film is at best described as an acquired taste. Grim, yes, arguably brilliant, yes, but it seemed that the general cinema-going public were growing tired of the kind of brutalised reality being offered to them. *This Sporting Life* and its financial failings were seen as proof by many that the fad for 'these kinds of films' was over. And while that may have been true, and the 'grim up North' shtick in less talented hands could be seen as meaningless rhetoric, what this handful of rather good films had done was to create a lasting legacy.

That legacy saw, for the first time, working-class Northern and Midlands voices being given a more rounded status in the previously cut-glass English stiffness of home-grown cinema. While these accents may have been heard before, in brief snatches or presented as comic or criminal, or stock character clichés, now it was becoming much more common to hear tones drawn out of the previously-ignored industrial heartlands. This was also partly due to the rise in popularity of bands like the Beatles, whose Liverpool accents became synonymous with the British beat group phenomena that swept across the globe. Northern-ness was not only accepted, it was also seen as sexy, funny, successful and more than human.

A Hard Day's Night (1964), Richard Lester's mock doc musical Beatles movie, in many ways owes as much to the previous run of kitchen sink dramas as it does to the lovable mop tops' own brand of 60s chart toppers. Not only does it nod towards the earlier films like *Saturday Night and Sunday Morning*, especially with its inclusion of old Arthur Seaton mucker Norman Rossington, but also in its employment of looser, more natural-sounding dialogue. The film works best when it appears to allow its famous protagonists to just run with their own voices. Though the film was scripted, it's the off the cuff-ness of the piece that holds it together and there are some dialogue gems amongst the rest of the film's often disjointed feel. The exchange between Ringo and an exasperated posh bloke on the train is worthy of Waterhouse's Billy Liar:

Man on Train: Don't take that tone with me young man,
  I fought the war for your sort.

Ringo: I bet you wish you'd lost

It was only a matter of time before more working-class voices began spilling onto the TV screens of a changing nation. In the winter of 1960 *Coronation Street*, originally planned as a thirteen-part series, landed in ITV's Friday night schedule. Initially focusing primarily on Bill Roache's Ken Barlow character, a young man who has been accepted into university and is finding his parents and his working-class roots something of an embarrassment, the show, despite early negative criticism, soon blossomed into a national institution.

'Talking of working classes… there's a show, that was all about that, [particularly] those early episodes. It was almost like a social documentary,' offered William Ivory when I interviewed him recently. Social documentary or not, it was and still is a hugely popular show. But in its early incarnation, it felt like a natural small-screen complement to those kitchen sink dramas or British New Wave productions. We can almost see a rudimentary version of Ena Sharples in Arthur Seaton's pellet gun target Mrs Bull, played by Edna Morris. Not only that, there is something about early Coronation Street, with its heavy dominance of female characters, which stretches back in time and channels earlier films. The Rovers Return snug scenes featuring Ena Sharples and her trio of eager gossips, including Minnie Caldwell and Martha Longhurst, echo those shadowy drawn parlour scenes from the film adaptation of *Love on the Dole*.

Other television productions were also beginning to reflect something of a more authentic working-class experience. Since 1954, writers Ray Galton and Alan Simpson had provided the scripts for Tony Hancock. *Hancock's Half Hour*, initially a BBC radio show, had turned its star into a household name. It became so popular that pubs would empty during its weekly broadcast. During its initial radio run, an episode later entitled *Sunday Afternoon at Home* perhaps provided the backbone of many modern sitcoms. The episode, which features excellent performances by not only its titular star but also Hattie Jacques, Bill Kerr, Sid James and Kenneth Williams, is brilliantly written. It's an immaculately honed comedy of emptiness, a fresh divination of that mournful and ridiculous time of the week. We feel Hancock's frustration, hear his irritation and laugh when his pomposity is pricked and his ego ends up being scraped away like so much burnt Yorkshire pudding from the dinner plate of life. The cast of characters are given little to do and they are all the more hilarious for it, the comedy is in the ticking of the clock, the silences punctuated by comfortless sighs and the deep, deep desperation that there has to be more to life than this. It was a format which would prove to be popular almost fifty years later when Henry Normal, Caroline Aherne and Craig Cash provided us with the sit-com *The Royle Family* in 1998.

Despite Hancock's success, undoubtedly helped by writers Galton and Simpson, the troubled star decided to cut them loose. It was just another in a series of questionable moves by Hancock that had seen the jettison of co-stars like Bill Kerr, Hattie Jacques, Kenneth Williams and eventually Sid James. He'd famously talked about 'getting rid of the rubbish' but what he failed to see was that much of the 'rubbish' was what had made him popular in the first place. While some of his changes in direction and personnel had worked, his most famous (and most loved) episodes such as *The Blood Donor*, *The Radio Ham* and *The Bedsitter* had been co-star free. However, it was difficult to see how getting rid of Galton and Simpson would ever cause him anything but harm.

It was at a meeting in October 1961 that Hancock informed Galton and Simpson he would no longer require their services. His own career began a gradual decline, ending sadly with his suicide in his flat in Sydney, Australia in 1968. Besides the scattered amylo-barbitone tablets and empty bottle of vodka were several suicide notes. One of them simply read 'Things seemed to go wrong too many times.'

Galton and Simpson, after parting ways with Hancock, were commissioned by the BBC to write *Comedy Playhouse*, ten half-hour plays on pretty much anything they desired. The series included episodes such as *Lunch in the Park*, starring Stanley Baxter, *Visiting Day*, with Bernard Cribbins and *The Channel Swimmer* featuring Bob Todd and a pre-Alf Garnett Warren Mitchell, but it was the fourth instalment, *The Offer*, which would go on to change television history.

The Offer proved to be so popular that it acted as the pilot episode of a brand new, soon to be long-running sit-com, called *Steptoe and Son*. The initial pilot episode and the subsequent series focused on the lives of a family-run rag and bone business comprising grizzled pensioner, Albert Steptoe, and his aspirational son Harold. It was a perfect storm of genius script writing, superb performances, incendiary social realism and (at times) heart-breaking pathos. The two lead performers, Wilfred Brambell (Albert) and Shakespearean actor Harry H. Corbett (Harold) proved to be an unlikely pairing — Brambell was a well-spoken gay Irish man, who took a more traditional approach to acting. Corbett, though, was serious and single-minded, he embraced modern techniques, and had worked closely with Joan Littlewood's Theatre Workshop. He also advocated the Stanislavski method of acting.

It was perhaps these obvious differences of age, experience and personality, coupled with the brilliant scripts of Galton and Simpson, that really brought the on-screen tension to life. In the basic set-up, Harold, an intelligent yet uneducated bachelor, pushing forty, is trapped by his manipulative father, a lazy and bitter man who has mastered the art of emotional blackmail. The hopelessness of their tragic situation is perhaps never captured better than in the original pilot episode. The episode ends with Harold threatening to leave the home and business, having received an undisclosed 'offer' of alternative employment. In a typical Albert move, his father refuses to allow Harold to borrow the horse to shift his gear. At the climax, Harold is driven to attempt to move the loaded cart by his own manpower. It proves to be an impossible task and before the closing credits roll Harold is reduced to a tearful broken man, rooted to the spot, trapped not just by his father's fear of loss but by his own fear of becoming something else. It's still a poignant moment and one that not only deals with private family tragedies but also with the injustices of position and social class. No matter what Harold wants to achieve, be it actor, round-the-world explorer or television repair man, it is simply too late, saddled as he has been with his aging relative and penny-pinched business. Any real chance of freedom has been hammered by his own sense of inadequacy, constantly reinforced by his father and a host of other walk-on characters who are quick to point out his lack of status. Harold is possibly the most tragic of all sit-com characters. Unlike Fletcher in the later series *Porridge*, his jailer is no prison guard, merely a frail-looking old man in a threadbare cardigan and tatty neckerchief, and there is no chance of parole.

While *Steptoe and Son* is undoubtedly hilarious, and the perfectly presented interchanges between father and son are immaculately constructed, it is the contradictions within class culture which define the onscreen dynamic. Albert, a stick-thin, weaselly character, an ever-present dog-end hanging limply from his toothless mouth, is always ready to point a grubby finger at his list of *Daily Mail*-invented targets.

He is the archetypal working-class Tory. Harold, by contrast is a socialist and self-appointed intellectual, gleaning his half-understood rhetoric from the handful of books he's picked up on the rounds. Their political differences are presented beautifully in an episode called *Tea for Two*.

> Albert: Every year more of the working classes are voting Conservative. It's getting really worrying for people like me. I mean, the class of person voting Tory now has gone right down the drain. It don't seem right that scruffs off the council estate are allowed to vote for gentlemen like Sir Alec.

> Harold: How you can sit there with your fundamental orifice hanging out the back of your trousers and talk like that I really don't know. I don't understand people like you. You get right up my shonka, you do. I mean, sometimes I just want to give up, I mean every time the Labour Party loses an election I want to give up. What is the point of keeping on struggling?

> Albert: You're a bad sport, rotten loser

> Harold: Dad, this isn't a game of cricket, our future is at stake.

Though political differences may have been a way for the writers to further explore the widening gaps between the two characters, as in the way they had exploited the generational and power inequalities, the episode doesn't seem forced. There appears to be a genuine appeal for change bleeding through the script, albeit in a comedic presentation. Corbett was certainly a Labour supporter, he had even made an appearance in a party political broadcast for Harold Wilson.

As the years passed Harold not only failed to get his chance at a better life but also his socialist utopia and, like Harold, we now all shift uneasily in a depressingly uncertain political landscape, as busy and as cluttered as the Steptoes' junk yard. Perhaps this is what makes the series so endurable.

Steptoe and Son ran for eight series and two feature films. It was only after an ill-advised stage tour of Australia (featuring a script not written by Galton and Simpson) that the actors, who had never really bonded, went their separate ways. Both actors were feeling increasingly trapped by their own characters and situations in a twist that mirrored their on-screen predicament. William Brambell outlived his on-screen son by several years, dying of cancer in 1985. Harry H. Corbett had succumbed to a heart attack in 1982, aged just fifty-seven.

While *Steptoe and Son* presented us with a grimy black and white version of the early sixties, things were about to get a lot more colourful.

7: What's It All About?

It seems to me if they ain't got you one way they've got you another.
So what's the answer? That's what I keep asking myself — what's
it all about? Know what I mean?

Alfie (1966)

Lewis Gilbert's *Alfie* (1966) begins with shots of mangy-looking dogs prowling around London's shadowy side streets with Waterloo Bridge half-glimpsed in the moon-washed background. It perhaps alludes to the mongrel make-up of the film's lead character, part working-class cockney, part aspirational opportunist, part dandy, part ruffian. But there is something more akin to an alley cat in the nature of Alfie Elkins — all shifty-eyed promise and unmistakable good looks. His metaphorical fur seems to bristle in the street light which illuminates his latest sexual conquest. For conquests they are; he lets us know this when he addresses us directly through the camera, referring to married woman Siddie (played by Millicent Martin) as 'it'. Excellently realised by Michael Caine, Alfie is less blond bombshell and more blond bombsite. The trail of destruction in his wake sends the pieces of broken marriage, unwanted pregnancy and abandonment spinning towards us in a hail of red-hot shrapnel. Yet for all this Alfie is a charmer. He is smart, witty and at times incredibly funny, albeit in an increasingly politically incorrect manner. Alfie is the encapsulation of every annoyingly handsome and untouchable reprobate we've ever come across either in school or workplace. The impossibly sexy, life of the party, all flashing smiles and winkle-picker shoes, well-groomed hard-on in a tailor-made suit.

Alfie, as with many of the films mentioned earlier, started life as a novel, written by Bill Naughton. He also went on to adapt his book into a stage play of the same name. In that play, at least in its initial run, Michael Caine, who became synonymous with that role despite the crappy remake, was nowhere to be seen. The lead in the original London production had gone to the Shakespearean-type John Neville, but it is a role that belongs to Caine. This is Caine at his beautiful best, before his later slide into Hollywood humdrum when he became famous for taking on pretty much any part as long as the price was right. (*Jaws: The Revenge*, anyone?) Here though, the actor *is* Alfie. The believability of the character is helped by the unconventional modes of address, particularly the director's choice of having his protagonist speak to the audience directly, looking straight to camera. The technique was also used effectively in the later John Hughes film *Ferris Bueller's Day Off* (1986), which was about another system-bucking rebel who eventually realises life and all its responsibilities is catching up with him. *Alfie*, on the surface, shares much with many contemporary mid-sixties productions, with its liberal use of comedy and employment of less-restricted sexual material. Parts of the story sit neatly alongside more throwaway sex-comedy fare such as the none-too-noteworthy *The Knack*, but it is clear that with Alfie there is a lot more going on.

Scratch the surface and we find ourselves looking at something far more engaging and deeply troubling. While *Alfie* appears to be all about sex, it is perhaps the by-product of sex — family (or usually lack of it) — which is what *Alfie* is really all about. In the film, there are constant references to absent or ineffective parenting, cobbled-together family units and one character even hints at parental abuse.

At the beginning of the film it is made clear that the title character has no time for family, when young Gilda refuses to steal from the couple she works for, explaining that they are just like family to her, Alfie admonishes her, saying that was precisely why she should steal from them. Though perhaps meant as a quip, there is something more loaded within Alfie's words — his determination to be independent, regardless of what that might cost him in terms of human relationships. This is brought tragically to bear towards the end of the film, and it leaves us wondering what kind of father figure had been around (or not) in his formative years to lead him down the path he has taken.

Though many of his actions seem deplorable by twenty-first century, post-#*metoo*, standards his unwillingness to see adult females as anything other than a homogenous 'it' places Alfie squarely in the un-PC 60s sensibility. Yet there is an unquestionable charm there, the character is inherently likeable and his need to keep himself happy, usually at the cost of others who fall directly into his path, is juxtaposed by his seemingly genuine desire not to make enemies or make anyone's life any worse than it needs to be. When Siddie makes some off-colour remarks about her husband, it is Alfie that seems keenest to keep him happy, and while this may be in his own self-interest it cannot be denied that Alfie appears to lack outright menace in his approach to life and relationships.

And if his stolid independence is, at least in part, admirable, his own cocksure spirit and worry-free existence seem to unravel as the plot moves on and he winds up in a state-run sanatorium. The reason for his incarceration appears to be physical. At a routine examination he is found to have an undisclosed chest complaint as depicted in the famous 'Shadows on me lungs' sequence, but it is clear that the mental anxiety caused by Gilda's decision to marry another man, taking Alfie's son away for good, is just as much a cause for Alfie to take stock and recover in the NHS establishment.

From this point on we begin to see Alfie as a more fragile prospect than his twinkly-eyed persona had led us to believe — although some of his classic behaviour continues, even in hospital, especially when he comically seduces a pretty young nurse, played by Shirley Anne Field, in a nice nod to *Saturday Night and Sunday Morning*, much to the chagrin of his miffed room-mate.

It is when Alfie is discharged from hospital that his problems really start and we start to see perhaps the beginning of the end of his philandering.

Alfie's inadvisable sexual liaison with his ex-room-mate's wife, Lily, when he offers her a lift home one Sunday afternoon, leads to one of the most heart-breaking and emotionally impactful scenes, not only in this film but in the entirety of 1960s cinema.

Illegal abortion, as mentioned earlier in this book, had already been touched upon fairly effectively in other films of this nature, but censorship and public opinion had meant any serious explorations into these back-street practices had been vetoed for more sub-textual approaches. While there is nothing visually explicit within Alfie's cinematic depiction, there is no doubt that the film's way of dealing with its sensitive subject matter hits us like a kick in the stomach.

When Lily, impeccably played by Vivien Merchant, meets Alfie at his temporary digs, where they intend to have the illegitimate child terminated, the film takes a sharp turn away from swinging 60s' mentality and the more jovial approach — only minutes before the film was in knockabout comedy territory, with its slapstick bar-room brawl, but it quickly descends into the type of realism we've examined in previous chapters, and it is that skilful juxtaposition which makes the abortion scene all the more jarring.

At one point the camera cuts away to an exterior shot which allows us to view the dingy diorama through a small rain-slashed window. Inside, the grim-looking bedsit, with its peeling wallpaper and grotty décor, replete with dartboard and half-drunk carafe of cheap Spanish plonk, seems to reflect Alfie's ham-fisted pretensions and inescapable working-class demeanour. The décor is made even more depressing by the arrival of Denholm Elliot's creepy and perfunctory abortionist. Alfie is equally pragmatic — while he is sympathetic to Lily's situation, he is unable to see what's happening as anything more than a mere financial transaction. 'My understanding of women only goes as far as the pleasure. When it comes to the pain I'm like any other bloke — I don't want to know.' Alfie's seeming lack of understanding when it comes to Lily's suffering is made clearer when he attempts to stifle her initial cries of agony as the procedure begins to take effect. She is literally made to suffer in silence.

We cut to Alfie, who now wanders the streets, having left Lily to fend for herself. 'I know it don't look nice, going on and leaving her, but what do look nice when you get close up to it?' His face perhaps shows more serious confusion than deep-seated guilt, the conflict of interests which at last seems to nag at his buried social conscience is made clear when he accidentally stumbles across the christening of Malcolm, the child he had with Gilda. Malcolm is now being raised by another man. Though the timing of christening/abortion is a narrative contrivance it is Lewis's adept use of contrasting imagery which helps to create the bleak montage. Though far from faultless, as an audience we can feel more than a modicum of sympathy for Alfie's predicament. Even when he enters the church, there is no connection. He appears ghost-like in the foreground. The church, and the celebratory nature of the occasion, is shot from a distance as if to underline Alfie's inability to reconnect with missed opportunities of the past. Whether it's his decision not to try and at least make a proper family with Gilda, or perhaps some unresolved issues relating to his own upbringing, Alfie is about to lose two children on the same day.

It is only after Lily has gone through with the termination, in the most painful and lonely of circumstances, that Alfie returns to the scene. And it is one of utter devastation, the devastation being in Lily's eyes. This is acting of its finest order. Merchant, who apparently only got the role at Caine's insistence, is incredible. The character, already fragile, is smashed to bits in a 'transaction' of Alfie's creation. The melancholy that creeps into the lines of a face that appears older than it should, settles into a blank look of murderous loss. But it is her strength that we are left with; she has dealt with this tragedy alone and for all of his swagger it is really Alfie who is at last able to see his weaknesses writ large.

Though warned by Lily not to examine the aborted foetus, which, thankfully, is never shown to the audience, Alfie cannot resist taking a peek. Perhaps it is his ego, his inbuilt need to check in with anything he may have created in his own image, no matter how pathetic or broken, or perhaps it is his morbid curiosity. Either way, we are given the opportunity to watch a man finally fall apart. It is a scene which is not easily watched and one that is even harder to forget. Alfie must pull apart some rather plush blue curtains in order to see the child. It is a moment which almost feels Lynchian in its drab theatricality. Just as Alfie has communicated directly to the audience in other scenes, now it feels as though he's breaking another fourth wall, one which will force him to come face to face with his own actions. Alfie's eyes may be on the foetus but ours are fixed on him and for a second we can see into his soul. Unlike the sharp suits he wears or the dolly birds he chases, it is not a pretty sight.

'I don't know what I was expecting to see, certainly not this perfectly formed being. I half expected it to cry out. It didn't of course, it couldn't have done. It could never have any life in it, I mean, not a proper life, a life of its own,' he recalls later to Nat (Murray Melvin), though it feels as though he is partly addressing his unseen audience again, this time with confessional intent. 'I thought to myself, you know what Alfie? You know what you done? You murdered him.'

Faced with the significance of his actions, Alfie appears to put his philandering ways behind him, and he settles into a relationship with the older Ruby (Shelley Winters). For once it is Alfie who seems to be at the mercy of another person's whims. Just as he has spurned Gilda and countless others in the past, he too now feels the casual rejection of a lover who has found a younger model.

Even Siddie, the married woman, who we first saw Alfie with in the opening scenes, is cold towards his fresh advances. Ironically, largely down to Alfie's past advice, she appears to have learned to love her husband again. And so, in a now infamous closing scene, an older, wiser man gazes once again to camera and asks 'What's it all about?'

Alfie is an extraordinary film — one of comedy, tragedy, sharp casual wit and deeply moving moments. Just as Arthur Seaton and company had shown us a different working-class experience of the North and Midlands, Alfie helped create the idea of a believable London-based working class, one which seemed to bury those 'lovable cockney' clichés of the post-war period. But more than that, it presented us with a beautiful character study of a man who is both of and out of his time.

In the next chapter, we will move away from the bright lights of the city and examine something much more rural.

8: Common as Muck

It ain't Jesus. It's just some fella

Whistle Down the Wind (1961)

The early 60s proved to be a strange and exciting period for cinema. In America, Audrey Hepburn became a visual icon in Blake Edwards' *Breakfast at Tiffany's*, *West Side Story* took Shakespeare's *Romeo and Juliet* and transformed it into a racially charged musical classic, Alfred Hitchcock rewrote the rules with his darkly grotesque shocker *Psycho*, and a deeply troubled Marilyn Monroe made her tragic final appearance in Huston's *The Misfits*. In Europe directors like Mario Bava and Georges Franju redefined horror with exquisite visual masterpieces like *Black Sunday* and *Eyes Without a Face*, while Jean-Luc Godard rode the French New Wave with his impeccably stylish *A Bout de Soufflé*. But more importantly than any of that, over in the UK, a young Hayley Mills was talking to Jesus in a cow shed.

Films like *Room at the Top, Saturday Night and Sunday Morning, A Kind of Loving* and *This Sporting Life* had presented us with a classic run of fleshed-out protagonists all working their way through a range of concerns and situations which UK filmmakers had scarcely even touched upon before. Whether it be the grinding existential angst of ruthlessly ambitious council employee Joe Lampton, the boozy brawling exploits of womanising Arthur Seaton, or the boatload of issues such as teenage pregnancy, mixed-race relationships and male homosexuality, which were explored expertly in Tony Richardson's *A Taste of Honey*, these were outings that sat stubbornly in the North or the Midlands. From Nottingham to Salford or the fictional construct of Dufton, these were dramas played out within the urban confines of the modern industrial landscape, one of small town and inner city. It was a world of smoke-filled pubs, dingy kitchens, factory floors, the back-breaking coal face and the relief of beer-fuelled weekends which clashed with the choking taste of clocked-in conformity. But while this may have been a refreshing glimpse into a working-class existence which had previously been dismissed, ignored or ridiculed, it still wasn't giving us the whole picture.

The rural side of working-class living has often been ignored in cinema. Working-class existence, even when more carefully explored in the films mentioned previously, or in later features, would invariably be linked to the city or small town, the term 'kitchen sink' seems to imply such, with its inescapable attachment to the British New Wave, *Coronation Street* or Ken Loach. But, in 1961, the Bryan Forbes film *Whistle Down the Wind* offered a beautifully-crafted glimpse into another side of that world, one of grassy hills, country paths, dry stone walls and the Second Coming.

Based on the novel of the same name by Mary Hayley Bell (though the cinematic version is shifted up north), *Whistle Down the Wind* is one of those rare films that seems to be adored by everyone. Mention this film and people's eyes will light up, there are some infinitely quotable scenes and the story's simple premise about a group of farm children who mistake an escaped criminal for Jesus Christ is both charming and brilliant. Filmed on location in the village of Downham, Lancashire, its country setting with its rolling hillsides, winding paths and crumbling farmhouses provides a contrast to the sooty, grime-ridden streets and workplaces usually associated with 'life up North', but the film is not afraid to drag us back to kitchen sink-style claustrophobia, with its shadowy barns and dimly-lit parlour rooms. Work too, is placed firmly within the film's visual narrative, like the Raleigh factory of *Saturday Night and Sunday Morning*, with its lathes and machines and relentless noise, here the daily grind is one of cowsheds, tractors and the squawk of distant crows.

Bernard Lee, a stalwart of post-war British films, probably best remembered for his portrayal of 'M' in the original run of Connery/Moore Bond films, is dad of the Bostock family and whilst he may run the farm, be the breadwinner and official head of the household, it is his hard-bitten sister Dorothy (Elsie Wagstaff) who is really in charge. No mention is made of the three children's absent mother but it is assumed that Mr Bostock is a widower.

The film opens with Eddie (Norman Bird), Mr Bostock's farmhand walking down to the river with a sack in his hand, the contents of which we can only guess. He is pursued secretly by the three Bostock children, Kathy (Hayley Mills), Nan (Diane Holgate) and Charles (Alan Barnes).

It is only when Eddie disposes of the sack in the water and is out of sight that the children come out from their hiding places. They fish the sack out of the river, and we see that the contents are three yowling kittens. It's an important opener that helps set up the film's main theme of faith which runs through the narrative, particularly the way in which faith for the sake of faith impacts on the lives of three naïve children. The potential 'cat drowning' scene helps ram home the message that bad things seem to happen all the time and God, or rather organised Christian religion, appears unable or perhaps unwilling to stop any of these incidents from happening.

The film is littered with instances where religious indifference or apathy is juxtaposed with that of unquestionable blind faith; whether it be the clueless Salvation Army officer, the well-meaning but pointless Sunday School teacher or the bad-tempered vicar who appears more interested in petty crime than getting to know his flock. The adults and their subsequent hypocrisies are laid bare before us. But the children at the heart of this piece are more forgiving. When met with various adults who are incapable of doing anything on any practical level to help them with seemingly simple tasks like re-homing a few unwanted kittens, for instance, their faith remains endearingly steadfast.

Even towards the beginning of the film, Kathy's initial cynicism as to whether Jesus will help them soon turns to remorse when she is chastised by her younger siblings for doubting the Good Book. Her belief in the Christian message is given a timely boost when the Son of God appears to be convalescing in a nearby barn. Jesus, of course, is an escaped convict, played by the gloomily sulky Alan Bates, whose bearded, shabby countenance and shadowy, shifty eyes only enforce the tension born out of the actual truth versus what the children want, or need, to be true.

For a while the joy or the fascination to be had with this film is the way in which the director plays with the idea of belief, and how these beliefs may change for worse or for better. The children believe that Jesus Christ has chosen them, but their beliefs are shattered when they learn the truth. Conversely though, Alan Bates' 'The Man' believes that the world is a bad place and just as the children's beliefs are altered, so are his, if only temporarily, as he manages to find unconditional love in the worst of situations. That is the miracle which the children have been seeking, and yet it is so earth-bound and without ceremony that they perhaps fail to see it.

There are many (some would argue mocking) allusions to the Christian story within the visual presentation of the text. When some of the children, who have been sworn to secrecy about the existence of Jesus, are harangued cruelly by the older village bully, there is a painful moment when a boy refuses to give up the knowledge he has, even as he's being physically tormented. It's clearly a reference to Peter's denial of his messiah, the only difference being that the cock-crows are replaced with the hooting of a distant diesel train. When 'The Man' reads falteringly from a story book to the assembled children, it plays out like a pathetically low-key Sermon on the Mount moment, and towards the end of the film as Alan Bates is arrested and held, his arms spread out horizontally in crucifixion fashion.

There are other moments too which give the 'reimagining' of the Easter story a down-to-earth working-class spin. In a touching scene which recreates the Nativity, the children (three of them, as in the three kings) offer the, if not newly-born, newly-discovered Jesus some simple offerings in keeping with the mindset of a collection of working-class kids. Nan, for instance, bestows on him a crumpled comic, replete with a free gift. The stable of the traditional story is swapped for a cowshed, the Last Supper changed to a simple birthday party and the Judas kiss replaced with a child's slipped tongue.

It's an effective yet simple story, the black and white photography beautifully realised by Arthur Ibbetson shifts effortlessly from arthouse, film-noirish cool to kitchen sink to family feature in a wonderfully well-lit, unmistakably British film which contains domestic charm and universal appeal. The dialogue is kept to a minimum and the performances Forbes draws out of his young cast are among the most memorable of that or any other decade.

Hayley Mills, daughter of John Mills and Mary Hayley Bell (author of the original novel), had already established herself at a young age with her appearances in *Tiger Bay* (1959) and Disney's *Pollyanna* (1960). She proved to be an even more precocious talent when it came to *Whistle Down the Wind*, which provided a refreshing contrast to her other film of that year, the truly cringe-worthy *Parent Trap* (1961). She plays the oldest of the three children, and it is her journey which we follow most closely. It is a journey which moves from the casual acceptance of faith because that's the done thing, to absolute belief, to shattering disillusion. While Kathy was at first the most reluctant to fall into the dogma of faith, she comes to accept it more fully than her siblings and is the one who is most let down by the revelations in the film's final moments. She is supported brilliantly by her younger co-stars, most notably by Charles, played by Alan Barnes, whose delivery of the line 'It isn't Jesus, it's just a fella' has fallen into cinematic history. It is the interplay of the three children which is at the centre of the film's appeal, the life they share, the secrets they conspire to keep and the common disappointment they encounter at the end of the piece. Their innocence and limited world view, encompassing all their naïve understandings of how the world works (or doesn't), is drawn briefly into the ancient light of an assumed messiah before being consumed by the shadow of modern doubt once again.

And yet despite the film not being a feel-good feature in the way that we've come to understand that term, it does provide us with something more substantial. Kathy, for instance, is left devastated not just by the final police siege and subsequent arrest of her idol, but by the realisation that she will have to make her own way in life and that her role models may take the form of more earthbound figures such as her father or her aunt. But we do feel hopeful at the end of the film. Though we are encouraged to share Kathy's disillusionment, as this makes our experience of the story more worthwhile, we also begin to feel that she has been freed from the constraints of false idols and petty Sunday school fabrications. Though her way ahead may be more complicated she may also end up being the guiding light that she has been seeking. It is a coming-of-age film in its true sense.

Whistle Down the Wind became the eighth most popular film in the UK and was nominated for several BAFTA awards. Bryan Forbes, who later made the altogether more disturbing *The Stepford Wives*, described it as his most popular and profitable project.

Whistle Down the Wind is undoubtedly fondly remembered and enjoyed by many, not just because of its innovative story, believable performances and deftly-handled script but also because of the way in which it brings together setting and situation so perfectly. And if Forbes's film at times edged towards the whimsical, another director was about lead the reality of inequality and working-class struggle crashing back through our TV sets.

9: Poor Cows and Kestrels

Casper, you make me sick, every lesson it's the same old story,
you've begged and borrowed and skived and scrounged.

Kes (1969)

Though he was describing *Cathy Come Home* (1966) when he talked
about 'A dramatic story to make your toes curl', Ken Loach, director and
outspoken critic of recent and not-so-recent government policies, might
well have been talking about any one of his numerous feature films. His
angry appraisals of a British system which seeks to attack the most
vulnerable members of our society have become honest observations of
modern life which sit uncomfortably with the cosier and blander
cinematic entries which pepper the UK film landscape. Anyone who has
seen the closing minutes of *Cathy Come Home*, replete with its shattering
revelation of a family being torn apart before our eyes, will understand
the kind of emotional punch that Loach is capable of delivering via his
form of polemic storytelling. *Cathy Come Home* was not just a television
play, it became a nationwide discussion leading to questions in the
House of Commons about the effectiveness or ineffectiveness of
government policy when it came to dealing with the problem of
homelessness. Fifty years on, in 2016, Loach caused similar controversy
with his film *I, Daniel Blake*. Its searing condemnation of the Work
Capability Assessment system and the crippling symptoms of Tory-
backed austerity proved to be an uncomfortable experience. Like *Cathy
Come Home* before it, Loach was keen to point out that the incidents
portrayed on screen were based on documented cases and the film was
once again an attempt, if not to change the system, to at least get a wider
audience talking about it. Of course, *I, Daniel Blake* became a target for
the kinds of people — journalists and politicians — who had a vested
interested in keeping the system just as it is. Predictably, *Daily Mail*
goblin Toby Young became one of the film's loudest and slightly
incoherent critics with his 'I'm no expert on benefits but...' method of
misguided attack.

Eighty-two-year-old Loach continues to direct, his earlier suggestions
of possible retirement now on the back burner with his next project
currently in production, and there is no doubt that his work remains a
stark reminder of societal inadequacy in the face of poverty, hardship
and inequality. Putting politics and controversy aside, it is clear when
we dip into his considerable back catalogue that he is and always has

been a skilled creator of some of the most beautifully-crafted films in the history of British cinema.

Born on June 17 1936, Ken Charles Loach was raised in the small northern Warwickshire town of Nuneaton by Jack and Vivien. His father, who had worked first in the pits then in the factory, wasn't, according to Loach in an interview given in Anthony Hayward's biography *Which Side are You On?*, his most ideal political role model:

> He took the *Daily Express*, which was a Tory newspaper, and probably voted Conservative. My mother would have done what he did. When I was fifteen they had a mock election at school and I stood as a Young Conservative, just because I read the newspaper that came into the house. Later I think my father became disillusioned with the management in his own factory, who he saw run it into the ground, so I think his respect for the ruling class diminished. He wasn't a strong union man though. Considering where he began, he had done rather well for himself and thought that, if he could do it, anyone could. It's a very flawed argument.

Loach was able to pass a scholarship exam securing him a place at the all-boys King Edward VI Grammar School. Though later Loach would look back critically upon that fairly arbitrary pass or fail system which saw many of his Secondary Modern counterparts denied routes into higher education and the benefits which ensued, it most certainly afforded him the opportunity of a better future.

That future saw him gaining entry to Oxford, but before he was able to resume his education he was forced to undertake two years of National Service. Stationed at RAF Syerston in Nottinghamshire, Loach quickly grew bored with his enforced military sabbatical and began to look for escape routes, albeit temporary ones.

Fascinated by theatre from an early age, the annual pantomime being his first introduction to acting and performance, Loach took advantage of the RAF's encouragement to undertake night classes and spent that time embroiling himself in the world of amateur dramatics at the nearby Nottingham Co-op Arts Centre (now called Nottingham Arts Centre).

After his National Service was over Loach enrolled at Oxford to study law. He soon found himself drawn more to the stage than the justice system. He was in several productions, became involved with the Oxford

Revue, and later understudied Lance Percival in *One Over the Eight*, starring Kenneth Williams. Later though, acting jobs dried up. Finding himself out of work, he decided to apply for a director's course at the BBC.

Loach was soon plunged into the chaotic world of directing live television with *Z Cars*, an innovative crime drama which ushered in a new way of depicting the police force, a long way from the tamer aspects of more traditional fare like *Dixon of Dock Green*. Loach's commencement of employment at the BBC chimed perfectly with the age. The Pill was available, the Beatles had helped not only change the face of popular music but had made more human northern working-class voices acceptable and desirable. On the back of this, British cinema had taken on a new honesty and grittiness with *Saturday Night and Sunday Morning* and *A Taste of Honey*, and rival ITV show *Coronation Street* was making other television programs seem hopelessly outmoded by comparison. The domination of middle-class voices and middle-England thinking — as represented by a more traditional BBC — was being railroaded by more tenacious and authentic perspectives.

> It's not a play, a documentary, or a musical, it is all of these at once. It is something new — but, more important, it is something rare. If you watch it we can promise you something that will stay in your mind for a long time.'

These were the words of Ken Loach's collaborator and producer, Tony Garnett, in the November 1965 issue of *Radio Times*. He was talking about *Up the Junction*. By 1965 there had already been two series of BBC's seminal *The Wednesday Play*. Its second series had included *Fable* — a disturbing examination of racism in modern culture, which subverted white domination for black in a neatly accusatory fashion. It was clear that the series was fulfilling its brief to provide the BBC with what head of drama Sydney Newman had described as 'agitational contemporaneity'.

Up the Junction not only fitted that brief, it *was* that brief and yet it was also, as Tony Garnett had alluded to, 'something rare', and it was out to do its own thing, using its own language, not just in terms of working-class naturalism but also in its look, feel and energy. Television was about to get its first real smack in the teeth.

The play, based on the stories in Nell Dunn's book of the same name, focused on the lives of a group of young female factory workers in

Battersea, detailing (and that is definitely the right word here) their working lives and nights out. Unflinchingly shot with lightweight 16mm film cameras, often on the streets or on location, a technique previously eschewed by the soundstage and studio-based BBC, it presented itself more as documentary than classic narrative or cosy drama. Audiences must have felt as though they were being dropped into the day-to-day experiences of a clutch of strangers. The voyeuristic nature and the unscripted feel made the piece appear new, disorientating and fascinating. The unabashed presentation of ordinary working-class citizens, stripped to the bone via a black and white, Italian neorealism-style lens, replete with unedited factory floor talk, boozy sexual encounters and a backstreet abortion, was more than enough to set the critics on edge and goad the likes of Mary Whitehouse into a spitting rage of fury.

But as impactful as that show was, its controversial fireworks faded quickly with the screening of the next Loach/Garnett collaboration. Originally titled *The Abyss* by writer Jeremy Sandford, *Cathy Come Home* went on, despite the assertions of *Wednesday Play* bosses Sydney Newman and Peter Luke that the series was not a political platform, to be one of the angriest attacks on government policy that British viewers had ever been witness to. It was television at its unobtrusive best, a jab to the guts, a brutal wake-up call fearlessly bringing to light the inhuman consequences of an uncaring bureaucratic system and its failures to address the problem of housing.

Cathy (Carol White), moves to London and meets Reg (Ray Brooks). They move into a flat together, with the understanding that there are no children allowed. However, Cathy falls pregnant and is forced to give up work to look after the child. Soon after, Reg is injured and cannot work. Forced to move in with Reg's mother, the tension builds and they move into another flat, where Cathy and Reg have two more children. On the death of their landlady they are thrown out by the bailiffs. And, as though the situation cannot get any worse, the story begins to unfold into a series of depredating and soul-destroying events which leave the family in pieces, separated by state and circumstance. The final moments of the film are incredibly difficult to process. Cathy, now homeless and estranged from Reg and family, has her children snatched from her by social services. Her hysterical cries of 'You're not having my kids' as they are rent from her desperate hands provide a wallop to an unsuspecting audience. The power of that moment cannot be understated. I saw the film a few years ago at a special screening at Broadway Cinema, Nottingham, and it still left patrons reeling, a blow that still wounds decades after its initial broadcast. Much of its intensity is born out of the way Loach approached the filming and direction, allowing the cameras to work around the action and actors rather than the other way round. He also let scenes play out to their natural conclusions, allowing ad lib and more realistic conversations to take place rather than trying to replicate a script. The famous final scene's agony is intensified because much of the anguish we see is real, Cathy's children are actually Carol White's own and when they are taken from her in that terrible climax at Liverpool Street Station, White wasn't aware of what was happening. The cameras had been placed at a distance from the action enabling Loach to capture a much more authentic response. This technique of ambushing actors with unexpected events or situations in order to create something which audiences find difficult to separate from reality was something the director returned to in later productions.

In the wake of *Cathy Come Home* and the political furore which it raised, particularly about the issues around homelessness and the draconian ways in which the system dealt with families in that situation, Shelter, the housing charity, was created. For a while at least many MPs would often cite *Cathy Come Home* as a sometimes-cynical means of political point-scoring, but Loach was guarded about that kind of attention. 'We were very suspicious of all those who tried to climb on the bandwagon… We saw Anthony Greenwood and he tried to pat us on the head, and we were not of a mind to be patted on the head; we wanted to draw blood.'

Cathy Come Home is relentlessly bleak, and that's the point. While it may have been the *cause célèbre* of various political figures at the time, there was little shift in real terms on the issues the film presented us with. As Loach himself said some years later. 'It changed virtually nothing in terms of the housing problem.'

This should not diminish just how good the finished film is. Its starkly depicted series of events unveiling the painful dismantling of a family is skilfully put together. Filmed in sequence, a technique Loach would continue to use throughout his career, its sense of immediacy and tragedy works its way horribly under our skin. Our own constructed political ideologies are called into question, petty disputes become irrelevant in the face of such human suffering. As disturbing as the picture is, it somehow brings the rest of us closer together, if only for its seventy-five minutes run time.

Loach followed up *Cathy Come Home* with *In Two Minds* in 1967. Another *Wednesday Play*, again produced by Tony Garnett, it was written this time by David Mercer. Dealing with the inadequacies of mental health provision, it was later remade as a feature film by Loach and retitled *Family Life* (1971). His first venture into feature film had been *Poor Cow* (1967), but it was his second cinematic offering that truly cemented itself into the hearts and minds of the film-going public.

Kes (1969) has lodged itself so firmly into the British psyche, both as a target of the highest critical acclaim and the daftest comic parody *à la* Vic Reeves and Bob Mortimer, that it is almost impossible to imagine it not being there. It almost feels as though it is now part of us, so familiar are its text and imagery. Billy Casper's often replicated two-finger salute has become shorthand for working-class rebellion and political disaffection. But as with most films that we cannot imagine being without, it was almost never there at all. By 1968 the more liberal era of the BBC was on the wane. Loach and Garnett quit the corporation to set up their own production company. They chose to adapt Barry Hines's novel *A Kestrel for a Knave*, naming their brand-new company Kestrel Films. The production was thrown into disarray when main backers National General, a Hollywood company, pulled their funding. Fortunately for Loach, kitchen sink stalwart and Woodfall Films captain Tony Richardson was able to wade in on Kestrel's behalf and managed to persuade United Artists to invest $400,000.

Kes tells the story of fifteen-year-old Billy Casper, who has been bored and demonised by a state school which saw him only as a scruffy inconvenience. Fatherless, ignored by his mother and bullied by his older brother, Billy finds himself staring into a no-option future of menial, back-breaking work. He finds escape from the bleakness of his ragged existence when he discovers and hand-rears a young kestrel. The symbolic nature of the bird, which swoops carelessly over the churning black smoke of the industrial landscape, high above the small town's dead-end streets, could not have been clearer, but if *Cathy Come Home* was designed to break us out of our cosy and complacent attitudes, *Kes* was designed to break our hearts.

With *Kes*, Loach began building on the approaches he had experimented with on *Up the Junction* and *Cathy Come Home* to present us with something more natural and real. Gathering together a host of non-professional actors who were local to Barnsley, the film's setting, Loach used as many real locations as possible. Much of the action, for instance, takes place in the then St Helen's School, its pupils making up much of the film's cast of extras and smaller roles. Loach also employed (as he would in many future productions) entertainers wrought from the Northern club circuit. Lynne Perrie, who would go on to play Ivy Tilsley in *Coronation Street*, played Billy's mother, and a young Duggie Brown was the milkman. Loach's attention to detail and ability to capture authentic voices and a 'lived experience' from Gryce, the rat-faced headmaster full of post-war regret and reactionary rhetoric, to the nervous library assistant unable to cope with Billy's snot-nosed curiosity and dirty hands, is uncannily representive of a time and place. Its realism only enhances the beauty and brutality of the piece.

The only professional actor in *Kes* was Colin Welland, who had worked on *Z Cars* alongside Loach. Cast as Mr Farthing, the only teacher at the school to exhibit more human qualities, he was also called upon between takes to act as educator to the young cast, to cement the real teacher/pupil relationship on screen. Welland had once worked at a school and his knowledge of the system added to the authenticity.

Brian Glover, a wrestler who went on to carve out an impressive career in television, film and stage, became the quintessential PE teacher in probably the film's most famous scene. Not so much a man as a lobotomised pit bull in a Manchester United footy shirt, Mr Sugden is the kind of rough-and-ready educator that many of us who were schooled in the 60s, 70s and 80s still have nightmares about. And if the football match represents a microcosm of a deeply unfair class-based system, where the less fortunate and unable are mercilessly picked last or left behind, then Mr Sugden makes for a tragically accurate depiction of the authority figures at the top of that system. In short, he is an abusive bully, arbitrarily changing the rules to suit his own purposes, and when we are presented with that unchanged reality we understand immediately the hopelessness of Billy's situation and that of millions of kids like him.

Loach's striving for on-screen naturalism, inspired by the techniques used in the Italian neorealism tradition, didn't always go his way, at least off screen, and some of his methods from that era would certainly be frowned upon now. In the caning scene, where Casper and some of his cohorts, including a younger, completely innocent child, are given whacks across the palms for their misdemeanours by a despotic headmaster, the cracks against the skin we hear and tears on the faces we see are real. Loach had instructed Bob Bowes, who played Gryce, to really 'go for it' when it came to dealing out the on-screen punishment, without the consent of the hand-throbbing cast. Loach's deception at first drew strong resentment from the boys, who immediately downed tools. They were only drawn back into the production when Loach bribed them each with some small change.

Some of the most marvellous moments in the film come when Billy, played by David Bradley, is alone with his precious kestrel. Beautifully filmed, the bird, often a black silhouette against a blue Barnsley sky, becomes a silent V-sign to all of Billy's troubles. We allow ourselves to believe, for a while, that everything will be okay. We share in Casper's awestruck appreciation of this small yet majestic animal — a flight-ready aspiration of hope.

> It's wild and it's fierce and it's not bothered about anybody. Not bothered about me, right. That's what makes it great. A lot of people wouldn't understand. They like their pets to be fussed. I'm not bothered about that. I just want her for her looks and to fly her. They can keep their talkin' budgies. They're nowt compared wi' her.

But when that hope is torn asunder in the film's climax, we are torn apart too. Jud, gruff and spiteful, bent out of shape by his lack of opportunity, vents his frustration on his mother and her string of boyfriends and his younger brother Billy. Like countless others he washes away the bitter taste in his mouth with copious amounts of alehouse bitter and gambles what's left of his wages on dodgy nags at the local bookies. In some ways, it's hard not to feel sorry for Jud. He is, of course, a victim of the same one-way contamination which blights Billy's life, but the vindictiveness he shows in the final reel of the film is hard to forgive.

When Jud leaves instructions for his younger sibling, already busy with school and two daily paper rounds, to place a bet for him, Billy, sensing the odds will not go in Jud's favour, spends the stake money instead. The would-be bet comes good and Jud is left severely out of pocket. 'I could have had a week off work with that.' Out on the rampage, Jud first goes to Billy's school and when he is unable to find him he stalks away with rage in his eyes. It is not until Billy returns home that we understand the full level of Jud's cruelty. He has taken Billy's beloved Kes, wrung its neck and left it in the bin.

The once-impressive bird is now a limp and lifeless shell, left to rot alongside old newspapers and dented baked bean tins. It's a fitting metaphor for Billy's own closed-in future of clanking mechanised dirt and disappointment.

Kes is a hard watch. Which isn't to say that it isn't funny or entertaining or expertly put together, because it definitely is, but the closing moments alone make it all the more challenging, and what's more the tragedy is bigger than a dead bird in the rubbish. As terrible as that image is, with everything it represents, we know that Billy's life, as crappy as it is already, is probably going to get worse, forced through a revolving-door existence of menial work and lack of opportunity, another nameless link in the cycle of constructed poverty, an easy target in an ideological war declared by the powers-that-be and a skewed education policy. As Loach says:

> The objective role of a secondary modern is to produce a certain amount of unskilled labour... The school and the youth employment officer cannot recognise that [Billy] has qualities, or they've got to find someone else to fill his manual job from the pool of eleven-plus failures.

Loach's most recent film, *I, Daniel Blake*, was undoubtedly important, shining a light on the government's shocking lack of humanity in failing to provide adequate financial support for those not able to work through sickness or incapability. It was expertly crafted and delivered its own fair share of gut-punching moments, such as the poignant food bank scene where malnourished mother Katie (Hayley Squires), weak with hunger, forces down a mouthful of cold baked beans out of the sight of her two young children. It was certainly a film which showed the world that Loach was still capable of raising the hackles of Parliament and the mainstream media. And yet I still believe *Kes* to be Loach's finest film to date. It's an elegant glimpse into a less than elegant situation. It is at once delightful but also messy and distressing, and yet it manages to be questioning without being preachy, angry without ever boiling into a rant. It is as honest and British and sensitive as you could ever hope a film could be. But more than that, it has gone beyond being a Ken Loach film — it's not his any more, it's ours.

10: The Criminal Class

I'm going to sit in the car and whistle Rule Britannia.

Get Carter (1971)

When gangster Jack Carter (Michael Caine) strides into a cheerless and poorly-maintained working men's club in the North-East of England, his spotless well-pressed suit, easy self-assurance and stony-faced determination set him apart from the more low-register customers of the dishevelled establishment. Dark and weary eyes view him suspiciously, calloused knuckles wrap around halves of bitter as a muffled juke box in the corner spills out a barely audible jaunty pop tune that mingles uncomfortably with the heavy presence of tobacco smoke and unimagined futures. When he orders a pint, he insists it comes 'in a thin glass' as opposed to the more usual pot-style container. This denotes not only a clever delineation between the north and south but also Carter's quick-witted readiness for violence in the blink of an eye attitude — his 'thin glass' can be used as a lethal weapon should things go array in the unwelcoming *mise-en-scène*.

The basic plot of Mike Hodges' *Get Carter* (1971) charts the grim journey of Jack Carter back to Newcastle. The city was once his home but all traces of his roots have been lost to his reinvented London gangster persona. He returns to attend the funeral of his brother and to discover the nature of his demise: '... the only reason I came back to this crap house is to find out who did it. And I'm not leaving till I do.'

What transpires is a gritty and brutal shadow-play of noirish deceit and betrayal encompassing murder, pornography, child abuse and a bloody revenge drama. In the end Carter, though in denial of his humble upbringing, cannot escape his past and he is left dead on a northern slagheap, the coal-black sea washing away his body as though it had never been there at all.

Get Carter remains a cold British classic, its nasty storyline populated by its flush of seemingly irredeemable characters is nevertheless gripping, if highly cynical. Lashed together by the clinical direction of Hodges and the icy characterisation of Carter, scored with the cool-as-fuck Roy Budd soundscape, the film has passed into legend alongside American crime dramas such as *The Godfather* (1972) and *Goodfellas* (1990). Like those films, many of its sequences and dialogue have worked their way into cinematic history. Its iconic images and snappy lines are now part of the movie landscape, but whereas a film like *The*

Godfather carries with it a certain untouchable, otherworldliness, *Get Carter* remains down-to-earth, a film that is almost too close for comfort.

Jack Carter, the working-class runt turned monied-up gangster, may have been more eloquently presented to us in the hands of Hodges but, in short, he was from a long line of cinematic guttersnipes done good (or bad, depending on your view of the law). For all his nods to a more cultured existence (when not engaging in more brutally violent activity), Carter can be said to have somewhat in common with the post-war spiv. Though largely now reduced to a single note stereotype, thanks in part to characters like Walker in *Dad's Army*, the spiv can be seen as a symbol of working-class entrepreneurial defiance and rebellion. Trevor Blackwell and Jeremy Seabrook in their book *A World Still to Win: The Reconstruction of the Post-War Working Class* describe the rise of the spiv as:

> … a symbol to those who might see their way to making big money out of a long history of privation and poverty of so many working people. He is also a reminder that many working-class pleasures have been illicit, and that the majority of working-class people have proved much more adept at learning to play the system rather than transform it.

The post-war spiv, at least on the silver screen, made for another handy shortcut to working-class over-simplified classifications. The distinctions between working-class characters seemingly only divided into three categories: that of the forelock-tugging conformist, the comedy character and the criminal. The first two categories were largely viewed as being the acceptable or 'respectable' working class, their promise by the end of the film to behave and knuckle down to the system would ensure they would live into another feature. The criminal, if he (spivs are always male!) was of a working-class background, would not fare so well as his more sticky-fingered officer-type contemporaries. The spiv certainly fell into the 'unrespectable' working class — the post-war version of the underclass if you will.

The character of Pinkie, for instance, in John Boulting's *Brighton Rock* (1948), is transformed from the shabby, neglected teen of Graham Greene's novel into a sharp-suited spiv-like character in the hands of a young Richard Attenborough. The spiv also surfaced in numerous films of the 40s and 50s, such as *It Always Rains on Sunday* (1947) and even in the form of two card sharks in Ken Annakin's strangely likable bit of post-war oddness *Holiday Camp* (1947). But although the spiv became a more antiquated idea by the 60s and 70s, he returned complete with new sales patter at the beginning of the 80s.

In 1981 a new sitcom, *Only Fools and Horses*, was aired by the BBC. Though the show has in its thirty-seven-year history become a 'classic' and David Jason, the actor playing its entrepreneurial hero has passed into the ranks of National Treasure, its first run of episodes hardly set the world on fire ratings-wise. Like the country's recently-elected new government, it would take a while for the programme to make an impression on the national psyche. In a way though, the show, created and written by John Sullivan (who earlier brought us *Citizen Smith*, about the comic escapades of a misguided Marxist), chimed with the changing attitudes of the UK. Socialism was now a dirty word and the nation was in the grip of the first wave of Thatcherism. The show's main character, a tax-dodging knock-off goods dealer, became the lovable poster boy for uncontrolled, I'm-all-right-Jack politics, a sort of 80s version of Harold Steptoe twisted cruelly by neo-liberalism and the fool's gold persuasion of the free market system. Some of the co-stars of that sit-com also appeared in John Mackenzie's *The Long Good Friday* (1980), a film whose protagonist, East End gangster Harold Shand (Bob Hoskins), became as reflective of the changing political face of Margaret Thatcher's Britain as Del Boy Trotter and co. would become.

The Long Good Friday began life as a script written by Barrie Keeffe called *The Paddy Effect*. Picked up by producer Barry Hanson and director John Mackenzie, the original treatment went through numerous changes, including having its title swapped for something less spoiler-filled, before it finally went into production. Even as the film was being shot, constant alterations were made to the script and set-up. Some of the key changes came at the behest of co-star Helen Mirren, who was unhappy with her original 'gangster's bimbo' character and casting. But the crux of the story and its themes remained in place. Shand, brutally bought to life by Hoskins, is the ruthless head of a gangland operation — the most powerful in London. Keen to become 'legitimate', perhaps echoing the concerns of Michael Corleone in Coppola's *The Godfather* series, Shand hopes to broker a deal with his American Mafia connections (in a twisted reflection of Thatcher's relationship-building with Reagan) and the city's key captains of industry and business elite.

Shand lays out his vision during a speech to the city's 'great and good' on his private yacht:

> I'm not a politician. I'm a businessman with a sense of history and I'm also a Londoner and today is a day of great historical significance for London. Our country's not an island any more, we're a leading European state and I believe that this is the decade in which London will become Europe's capital. Having cleared away the outdated we've got mile after mile of land for our future prosperity...

The speech, mirrored later in the film in his closing address to two Americans, shows Shand at his pompous best and worst. His loud-mouthed patriotism, underscored by barely-concealed hypocrisy and right-wing political bias, is apparent. His talk of clearing away 'the outdated' gleefully sums up the recent battering that the Labour Party and socialism had taken at the hands of Thatcherism, and his spiel about 'our future prosperity' seems only to apply to the privileged few lucky enough to be invited the party, those literally and metaphorically 'in the same boat'. His eagerness to make new relationships with foreign nations, particularly European ones, only seems to stretch as far as money-making, as his vicious form of racism, aimed largely at the Afro-Caribbean and Asian communities that occupy the run-down ghettos of his manor, is apparent.

His plans, including the wining and dining of two American Mafia representatives, go awry when his firm becomes the target of a series of bomb attacks. When it becomes clear that the onslaught has come at the behest of the IRA, Shand's typically bloody-minded, unsuccessful counterattack provides an allegory for the way in which governments then and now fail to deal with terrorism. Keeffe presents us with a story wrapped around the concept of what happens when capitalism comes face-to-face with a non-shifting form of idealism.

But for all of its social commentary, the film is also fantastically entertaining. Speeding motors, shooters, gangland murders and the film's rollicking pace meant that it appealed to the same audience who had followed the likes of Jack Regan in ITV's long-running cop show, *The Sweeney* and who were also lapping up new shows like *Minder* and *The Professionals*. From the gloriously 80s theme tune, to the razor-sharp dialogue which seethes with humour and menace — 'Well, let's put it this way. Apart from his arsehole being about fifty yards from his brain and the choirboys playing 'unt the thimble with the rest of him, he ain't too happy.' — it's remarkably addictive viewing. It's a beautifully-made piece which manages to be both an example of early 80s cinema which is absolutely of its time, and something deeper, which resonates with twenty-first century relevance.

The film did not enter into screen history without its problems. Though created for the cinema, *The Long Good Friday* was financed by Black Lion, a subsidiary of Lew Grade's ITC Entertainment. As such, it was commissioned to be shown on ITV. Grade, fearing that the film was a 'glorification' of the IRA, insisted on substantial cuts. Bob Hoskins had learned that they were going to replace his voice with that of another actor for the film's US television release. This led to Hoskins suing the distribution company, preventing its broadcast on American networks. With the film facing many cuts, rendering it barely intelligible, George Harrison's company Handmade Films bought the rights back from ITC and the film was finally given a theatrical release, unhampered by censorship.

Much of *The Long Good Friday*'s brilliance is down to Hoskins — as Harold Shand he delivers an incredible performance. We witness his delusion of being a 'respectable' business man only to see that respectability devolve quickly into barbarism at the first hint of trouble. In a famous scene, Shand, not yet realising he is up against the IRA, hauls in his rivals in the dead of night, hanging each of them upside-down from meat hooks in a back-street slaughterhouse. Even then, when his brutal form of control is evident, he still clings to the idea of being legitimate, having earned his place at the more respectable boardroom tables where he imagines himself present.

Shand is a fascinating man, both simplistic and complicated, violent and sincere, immediately likeable and repellent. For all his faults though, we can't help but feel some remorse when he is captured and driven away to face an undignified death at the hands of his enemies.

Mirren too, adds a touch of class. At first her character had been a much more throwaway 'bit of skirt', an empty-headed moll, eye candy for the Saturday night picture crowd. But after much wrangling and rewrites of the script, the character of Victoria became not just Shand's sexual partner but also his business partner. Her private school upbringing and posh silver-spoon credentials contrast sharply with Shand's working-class beginnings but her clear intelligence and connections to the landed gentry become yet another important piece in his supposed legitimisation. Though on the face of it their relationship seems strong, it is suggested that it is a calculated form of love based on the exchange of power. Although Victoria provides level-headed counsel we are left feeling that she will betray Shand the moment a more powerful proposition comes along.

Shand's grass-roots level army-like subordinates present us with an interesting, if slightly simplified, view of class and class structure. Here we have a group of men who are as intelligent and as brilliant as their 'privately educated' counterparts, but whereas those people have ended up as boardroom leaders or politicians, Shand's men have had to seize power by other less legal means. And yet, though there is much talk of loyalty in this particular criminal underworld, there is little of it on show in *The Long Good Friday*, certainly not from Shand himself, who despatches Jeff, his right-hand man and 'son' figure, in a moment of violent insecurity. Shand's acts of vengeance appear to be born more out of desperate self-preservation than from genuine allegiance. There is also no loyalty when it comes to Shand's handling of the residents of his beloved communities, particularly if they happen to get in his way or are the wrong skin colour. Indeed, arguably, one of the problems *The Long Good Friday* might have faced then (and possibly now), from an artistic point of view, was that Shand with his misplaced patriotism, wealthy trappings and sneering racism became not the intended ogre but a kind of hero to some. At the time the National Front was on the rise, the Brixton riots were just around the corner and racial prejudice was alive and well in workplaces, schoolyards and on our television screens. The UK was a while away from more liberal approaches and the political correctness which would prevail later in the decade. Sitcoms like *Love Thy Neighbour* and *Mind Your Language*, with their pervasive racial stereotyping, were still fondly regarded by many. Even the aforementioned *Only Fools and Horses*, with its early-episode references to 'Paki shops', reflected the nation's casual approach to anti-black and Asian feeling.

The Long Good Friday not only became a fitting successor to the previous decade's *Get Carter*, it became a British cult classic in its own right, laying the groundwork for future home-grown crime thrillers such as *Lock, Stock and Two Smoking Barrels* (1998), *Snatch* (2000), *Sexy Beast* (2000) and *The Business* (2005). There is something deeply satisfying about revisiting the film. For all of its intelligence it is an enjoyable crime caper, gritty, dark and sublime. It's beautifully acted, brilliantly shot and a lot of good fun. But as the old saying goes, crime doesn't pay, and in the next chapter we will examine how young working-class men and women were paying the price at Her Majesty's pleasure.

11: Teenage Wasteland

When you're part of a gang, you soon find the parts of you that don't fit. These apparent defects can become assets; they're the things about you that make you interesting & useful.

Pete Townshend

In the late 60s, radical dramatist Joan Littlewood was having a spot of bother with some local delinquents. Her stomping ground, the Theatre Royal, Stratford East, was the target of a gang of youths who repeatedly vandalised the exterior, mugged unsuspecting actors and offended the delicate sensibilities of the steady stream of middle-class punters who frequented regular performances. Littlewood's response to this hostile takeover was not to batten down the hatches but to leave them wide open. In an innovative and unexpected move, she invited the bunch of young reprobates in. At first the boys were employed to shift gear around and carry out more practical tasks but eventually Littlewood began to work with them in more theatrical terms. She was able to coax performances from the gang members using improvisational techniques and structured workshops. These unconventional workshops drew the attention of Notting Hill-based film-maker Barney Platts-Mills. To the teens, Platts-Mills may as well have come from Mars. His decidedly posh artiness and flash of acid-dazed bohemia clashed awkwardly with their rather more down-to-earth experience of petty crime and poverty on the not-too-prosperous streets of East London. Unperturbed, Platts-Mills set out to make a documentary portraying the work being created by Littlewood and the local youths. Eventually the young crowd came to accept the director, if not chiming with his upper-class credentials, at least recognising his streak of rebellion which perhaps reflected their own.

The resulting film, *Everybody's an Actor, Shakespeare Said*, a sort of half-hour fly-on-the-wall piece, which captured improvised moments, reflecting the boys' lives and their inner fantasies, is a fascinating document which neatly captures the era and provides an interesting companion film to the earlier *Free Cinema* offering, *We are the Lambeth Boys*. Spurred on by the gang's request that he should make a feature film with them in it, Platts-Mills used his connections to raise £18,000. With it he proceeded to make what would become *Bronco Bullfrog* (1969).

I first came across *Bronco Bullfrog* thirty-odd years ago, when I was made to watch it at school. While I appreciated that it kept me from attending yet another boring English class, I think it's safe to say that its unpolished rawness did not immediately appeal to my fifteen-year-old self, who at the time would have been much more enamoured by the glossy Hollywood shlock of the latest *Nightmare on Elm Street* sequel. Watching the film again more recently, it is that same rawness which now appeals to me. One might look at the film as a stepping stone between *The Loneliness of the Long-Distance Runner* and late 70s entries such as *Scum*, *Quadrophenia* and the 2006 film *This is England* by Shane Meadows, but to see it merely as a stop-gap would be unfair, as the film is remarkable and its merits place it firmly within the ranks of other overlooked classics.

The simple story focuses not on the titular character, but on Del Quant (Del Walker), an apprentice welder, and Irene (Anne Gooding), his round-shouldered teenage girlfriend, who fall for each other and unsuccessfully attempt to run away together. It is related to us in such a beautifully matter-of-fact manner that it is easy to forget we are watching a fully-fledged drama and not another Platts-Mills fly-on-the-wall documentary.

Bronco Bullfrog, AKA Jo Saville (Sam Shepherd), is the one character in their lives who offers them an escape, albeit a temporary one, from their overbearing parents and bleak, empty locales. Del's future, or lack of it, is presented on the deadened face of his haggard-looking work foreman, whose only enjoyment is derived from staring into overcast skies in search of his beloved homing pigeons. And in an exchange where Irene's mother enquires whether she has homework to do, her daughter's quick response of 'They don't bother with the likes of us' allows us a glimpse into the kind of educational rigour that was applied to non-grammar school working-class girls of the period — good for the factory, shop work and little else.

While Del has already dabbled in minor law-breaking activity — the robbery of a café, where the only pickings to be had were nine pence and a handful of cakes — Bronco has recently been released from Borstal and seems eager to re-engage with his criminal lifestyle. Unlike Del though, he has his eyes on much bigger rewards than Mr Kipling and small change. Putting together a small gang, including Del, he sets about robbing a train carriage full of household goods, kitchenware and bed linen, with the intention of selling it on. Though the job seems to go smoothly, despite a close shave with a night watchman, the police get wind of the operation and are soon on the trail of Bronco's mini-crime wave. Irene and Del briefly find freedom in Bronco's flat but their liberation comes crashing to a halt when the law turns up and the three find themselves on the run with nowhere to go.

The non-professional actors, many of whom also appeared in *Everybody's an Actor, Shakespeare Said*, are perfectly placed in this semi-scripted, semi-improvised snapshot of a late 60s disenfranchised culture. Characters and their seemingly inescapable realities are brought starkly to the fore, the limitations of their presence underscored by the suffocating nature of their environments, including tired-looking tower block flats, cramped terraced houses, grotty greasy spoon cafés or the narrow passage of the underpass where Del is handed a beating by a rival gang. The dimness and smallness is depicted effectively by the crisp black-and-white cinematography of Adam Barker-Mill, and it is the claustrophobia of the protagonists' situation which leads to the sense of abject frustration and outbreaks of casual violence. But even the violence seems apathetic. Half-hearted fists connect limply with bodies which are already waving their arms in submission, as if fights and their build-ups only seem to happen to while away another hour or so between clocking off time and bed.

And yet within this there is also humour and well-placed banter. The natural chemistry between the teenage cast is evident and the dialogue never feels forced. The male members of the gang look the business, rolling as they do off the back of the original wave of Mod. By the late 60s, many Mods had rejected the more psychedelic art school nature of the image for something more solid that didn't necessarily carry the harder edges of the skinhead look. The look here is impeccably portrayed. There is a beautiful scene where Del, Irene and Bronco get drunk at the flat and Bronco is dressed in all of his knock-off finery — impossibly tight sta-prest trousers, matching paisley tie and high-collared shirt, shiny Doc Marten boots and wide white braces. Somehow, despite his drunken slurring, he owns the room. His inebriated demeanour and his snazzy attire clash awkwardly and perfectly like a low-rent Corleone or Harold Shand's gormless younger brother.

No matter that *Bronco Bullfrog* remains far less famous (or infamous) than *Quadrophenia*, *Scum* or *Kes*, it is still one the best depictions of post-war, pre-punk urban disillusionment and it offers an unapologetic, unromantic study of a working-class younger generation who are both beaten up and beaten down.

A few years later, up in Scotland, Bill Forsyth had begun collaborating with his own gang of young actors at The Glasgow Youth Theatre. The group, which included Margaret Adams, Danny Benson, Robert

Buchanan, Drew Burns, Gerry Clark and John Hughes, was already well versed in the art of performance, sketch building and 'making it up as they went along'. They were keen to work with Forsyth, though they were at first sceptical of his designs to make a film with them in it.

Gregory's Girl (1981), an idea initially developed out of scripted scenes and the quirky improvisations of his precocious cast, had drawn the attention of the British Film Institute (BFI). For a while at least it seemed a shoo-in to receive the financing it required to get off the ground, but the funding never transpired. Although at first disappointed, the BFI's decision causing some considerable bitterness, Forsyth, with the agreement of his youthful cast, set about making a different film, for which he raised the money himself. In a decision which today seems both laughable and heart-warming, the director began making a movie on a budget of just £2000, an amount which would have even poverty row hacks like Ed Wood crying into their angora sweaters. Forsyth was able to raise this micro-budget by begging for cash from local businesses, trade unions and the like. He was successful too, prudently approaching potential funders in the guise of not a film-maker but a social worker.

That Sinking Feeling (1979) is a comedic heist movie, whose protagonists are not the sharp-mouthed, good-looking gangsters of Hollywood crime movies, but a bedraggled and spotty gang of Glasgow teens who set about planning the robbery of ninety sinks from a nearby factory. What unravels is a simple story incorporating the planning and buildup, then the actual caper and its aftermath. It is a story which has been told many times before, and yet its method of delivery, blessed as it is with Bill Forsyth's style and humour, makes it a refreshingly entertaining piece of knockabout comedy, albeit tinged with the bitter whiff of urban deprivation.

The film, though lacking the earnestness of other more po-faced realist dramas, never flinches from showing us the reality of living on the breadline in late 70s Glasgow. Its gritty *mise-en-scène* of rain-soaked parks, mould-ridden bedsits, demolished houses and boarded-up factories ensures that our gaze is never completely drawn away from the many examples of multiple social deprivation, and yet in the hands of Forsyth, the grimness is tempered with what would become his stock-in-trade form of quirkiness and gentility.

Darkly comic humour runs throughout much of Forsyth's work, including *Gregory's Girl* and *Local Hero* (1983), but with *That Sinking Feeling* we get to see that style forming before us, and it could be argued that the film acts as a dry run for his more polished features. And yet there is something so wonderful about how this low-budget film hangs together with its experimentation, sketch-like structure and bizarre little set pieces, that it becomes a near-classic in its own right.

Though not all of the gags or reveals work in the film — occasionally the humour strays into 'you had to be there' territory — for the most part it's a clever and slightly surreal triumph which seems to riff as much on Billy Wilder as it does on Ken Loach. Right at the start of the film, the black and white title *That Sinking Feeling* literally sinks down the screen. Moments later we are treated to main character Ronnie (Robert Buchanan) performing an eloquent soliloquy in the dismal torrential rain; mud and damp soaking into his unwashed jeans. He berates a statue of Field Marshall Earl Roberts, wondering how he'd managed to achieve so much, when he didn't even seem to have the two O-levels that Ronnie has worked hard to gain, in a pre-Rab C. Nesbitt bit of half-baked philosophy. The scene ends when Ronnie, kicking the park bench in frustration at not having a job (despite his educational prowess), disturbs a tramp who has been trying to sleep through the teenager's ranting and raving. It's a clever kind of reveal that helps set up the tone of the remaining film. Throughout its run-time the piece eloquently mixes social realism with more fantastic elements — this *modus operandi* is underlined on a title card which appears on screen as the film begins:

> The action of this film takes place in a fictitious town called GLASGOW. Any resemblance to any real town called GLASGOW is purely coincidental.

In another scene which demonstrates this idea perfectly — highlighting both the grottiness and the abject absurdity of their situation — three characters huddle for shelter in a car as the ever-present rain hammers down. Though perky and almost matter-of-fact in their tone, the youths discuss the various ways in which they could end their lives, their upbeat nature juxtaposing rudely with their seemingly unending misery. 'There's got to be more to life than suicide,' one of them states. As the scene ends the camera pulls out to reveal that the car they are sitting in is broken down and on bricks.

But it's the hope that the protagonists cling to which makes them most endearing to us. They hardly ever stop to complain, instead they continue to make their big plans. In one moment Wal (Billy Greenlees) thumbs a travel brochure picking out an exotic holiday, seemingly unaware that his toes are sticking out of his knackered plimsolls. The film also takes us down some odd little avenues. There is the silly faux-science fiction subplot, for instance, involving an amateur chemist gang member, a home-made knockout drug and a sleeping victim 'not due to wake up till 2068'. There are also some respectful nods to *Some Like it Hot* — when one of the small-time crooks takes to dressing up as a girl as decoy during the main raid, this leads to him becoming obsessed with female attire, lengthily debating the merits of grey or brown tights with his exasperated girlfriend. And if all this sounds like a hodge-podge of ideas, that's because it is, but it works just as well because of that and the quirkier elements help to ensure the film's lasting cult appeal.

In the absence of money or any of the normal attributes that go with a comfortable existence, the characters seem to draw heavily on the only resources at their disposal — wit, good-natured banter and charm. At the beginning of the film Simmy dupes an unwitting sales assistant out of a cigarette by promising to purchase a music centre he has no way of ever being able to afford. Like the big robbery later on, it's done without any real malice, it's simply a cheeky act of temporary survival.

Like the Ken Loach films which had come before it and the Shane Meadows films which would follow, *That Sinking Feeling* wears its political and humanistic qualities on its rather tatty-looking sleeve, but it's also much more than that, it's an oddity and a slice of eccentric Scottish wit and wisdom, both heroic and down-to-earth at the same time. It may be able to eloquently and subtly dismantle larger issues and the errors of free market capitalism within an entertaining context, but it also is never afraid to focus on the minutiae and mundanity of modern living. It may be waving two fingers in the air with one hand, but it's scratching its arse with the other.

1977 was not a good year to try and stick it to the Home Office over its draconian continuation of short sharp shock, Borstal institutions, particularly when you were the BBC and were seeking a TV licence fee rise from that very same department. And so, the original version of *Scum*, directed by Alan Clarke, was unceremoniously banned.

Clarke, who would later become synonymous with hard-hitting and often confrontational film and TV productions with a CV which included *The Firm*, *Pendas Fen* and *Made in Britain*, had begun life on a different path. As a child, he had gained a place in grammar school, which in turn had led to a steady job as an insurance clerk. But he later turned his back on this stability when he emigrated to Canada to take on work in a gold mine. Later he enrolled on a course in radio and television and pretty soon he was back in the UK, and by 1969 he was cutting his teeth as director on the BBC's *Play for Today*.

The Wednesday Play, later renamed *Play for Today*, proved to be an incredibly important series in the history of British television. It launched the careers of Mike Leigh and Ken Loach and introduced viewers to challenging and original productions such as *Abigail's Party*, *Nuts in May*, *Blue Remembered Hills*, *Cathy Come Home*, *Up the Junction* and *The Black Stuff*, which would later be adapted into the six-part *Boys from the Black Stuff* series.

Scum, though, written by Nottingham-born Roy Minton, was one of only two *Play for Today* presentations to be prohibited by the BBC itself, the other being Dennis Potter's decidedly nasty domestic drama, *Brimstone and Treacle*.

Despite Clarke's adherence to suggestions of cuts — a suicide was removed and a scene where a warder voyeuristically gazes over the sexual abuse of an inmate was shortened considerably — *Scum* was dragged from the schedules just as young Carlin's battered, bleeding body was dragged down the wing's corridor at the denouement of the play. According to producer Margaret Matheson, the delayed broadcast, followed by the outright ban, had been brought about by internal BBC pressure rather than outside forces, but it would be naïve to think that the Home Office wouldn't have been happy with the decision.

Scum wasn't unleashed on the public till 1991, when Channel 4 showed the piece as part of its season of programs on censorship. Despite the political machinations, it's easy now to see why boardroom types might have baulked at broadcasting *Scum*. Centring on the brutality and 'reality' of a typical Borstal, the play focused on the 'one-way contamination' of a flawed judicious system, especially when it came to the rehabilitation and treatment of young offenders. Roy Minton had researched the topic thoroughly, even spending time in a Borstal. He thought it important that what he was portraying on screen was reflective of what was happening in reality. Within the deeply scathing narrative, the cast of unfortunate teens is thrown into an authoritarian nightmare, lorded over by uncaring custodians and the likes of 'Daddy' Banks, who is quickly usurped in a vicious attack by Carlin (Ray Winstone). It's a *Lord of the Flies*-style presentation, violent and achingly political. But what distances it from that text is the element of class.

While the protagonists of the aforementioned book are largely middle-class, the inhabitants of the young offender's unit are certainly all working-class. Like the public school of Lindsay Anderson's *If...*, the Borstal in *Scum* becomes a handy microcosm of society and the inmates occupy its lowest place. Its commentary about the social order (or disorder) could not be clearer. Institutional racism, the adult abuse of children and the brutalising corruption of power all weigh heavily in the unsettling drama, which can only ever end as it does in a climax incorporating riots, gang sodomy and suicide.

Though shelved by the BBC, the project was given a new lease of life two years later when it was picked up by producer Don Boyd for a ready-made theatrical version. It was ready-made in that it largely borrowed from its original casting and followed the original's structure closely. While the 1977 TV version still retains a certain power, which can now be enjoyed on its DVD release, the 1979 theatrical incarnation is more finely tuned. The actors who were carried over from the first version definitely appear sharper in the second production, as though they'd had time to really get to grips with their roles. Where key actors were replaced, as in the case of David Threlfall, it feels like an improvement, which is not to besmirch Threlfall's original performance, but Ford is simply magnificent as Archer in this version. Clarke, a strict task master when it came to directing *Scum*, drilled his young and largely inexperienced cast as though they were training for the Olympics. But his actors grew to respect him, chiming with his earthy, down-to-earth 'no bullshit' personality.

Minton though, who had largely been left out of the process of turning the play into a theatrical film release, had been unhappy with some of the changes made to his original script. One of the key differences had been the removal of some of the more homosexual content. In the 1977 version, Carlin is seen to adopt a young male inmate as his 'Mrs'. According to Minton, the scene was an accurate representation of a common practice both in young offenders' units and adult prisons, and he believed it was important as it also helped to humanise the often-violent young inmate. The cuts and alterations to the script led to a falling-out between Minton and Clarke and the two never recovered their once-good friendship, though Minton did visit Clarke when he was later dying of cancer.

Despite Minton's reservations, the cast delivers some near-perfect performances, Ray Winstone is appropriately hard-edged and charismatic as Carlin, while rat-like Phil Daniels as Richards is at his nasty snarling best, as a deeply unpleasant Daddy's bully boy who is cut down to size by a billiard ball in an unwashed sock. Mick Ford brings an intellectual charm to his portrayal of Archer, an educated miscreant, who, after being caught with his hand in the till and sent down, uses his understanding of 'the rules' to overcomplicate life for the dim-witted wardens and Bible-bashing governor.

> ... I've got to save myself despite whatever methods you bastards devise to destroy me. I'll get through it, or I won't, but it's my way... the punitive system does not work. My experience of Borstal convinces me that more criminal acts are imposed on prisoners than by criminals on society.

And while it is easy to get caught up in the violence and degradation it is also a brilliantly put-together piece of work. Take the famous scene of Carlin's take-over of the wing. After he has dealt with Richards, leaving him bloodied and unconscious on the rec room floor, he moves down the corridor, up the stairs and into the toilets where he quickly dispatches the unsuspecting Banks. This sequence, captured in an unbroken take, is masterfully done. Not only is it technically stunning, it also helps galvanise Clarke's documentary style, a style which helps us to forget we are watching a fiction and leads us to believe we are dealing with an immediate reality. The intelligence of the scene is underlined by an earlier section in the film. Previously, we have been introduced to the rec room and the trainees' association time, and in a first viewing of *Scum*, this could be seen as narrative filler, a chance for the audience to acquaint themselves with some of the characters and the layout of the place. But subsequent viewings and a deeper understanding of the film show us that Clarke is cleverly placing us into the mindset of Carlin. Carlin is not simply surveying his surroundings, he is scoping out his future crime scene, planning his carefully-laid trap. This all helps with the roundness of his character — this is no mere thug who wins out purely because of brute force, this is a young man who has been forced by an unfair system to become a calculating and cunning criminal. This is not about power, it's about survival.

Though the film clearly takes an angry and political swing at a problem deeply embedded within the late 70s state of affairs, particularly when it came to crime, punishment and inequality, the film also owes much to *The Loneliness of the Long Distance Runner*. The violence may be more horribly depicted and the climax grimmer, but what's being said is simply a louder and somewhat less poetic version of what was spilling from the lips of Colin Smith fifteen years earlier. And while Smith was clearly the focus of our concern, his stock-in-trade kind of rebellion is perhaps split over several characters in *Scum*, namely the largely in control Carlin, the intelligent Archer and the weaker victim of a wider society, Davis. As much as *Scum* stands alone as a piece of (then) modern cinema, mementos of Sillitoe's earlier adaptation are spat across the bleak grey walls. But it is an outstanding piece, both versions are masterfully adept at cutting through literary pretensions in order to present us with something much more fierce and honest. The final moments of *Scum* present us with a minute-long silence for the recently-deceased Davis. The camera focuses on the warders and governor who stand shoulder to shoulder in defiance, complicit in their corruption which has contributed heavily to this tragedy. It's a starkly symbolic reminder of just who's in charge — a brutalised minority of uncaring, unseeing men who lord it over a sea of forgotten, interchangeable faces. It's real, it's horrible, it's us and them.

The formula was repeated later on in 1982's *Scrubbers*, a film by Swedish actor and director Mai Zetterling. Set in an all-female Borstal, it's an interesting piece which sits neatly alongside *Scum* and features some excellent early performances by Pam St Clement and Kathy Burke, but it feels uneven and never touches the same nerve as its predecessor. David Mackenzie's 2013 film *Starred Up* compared more favourably, it riffed on some of the same themes as *Scum* and certainly channelled some of its passion and brutality, but it also added its own dynamic with its mix of prison drama, social commentary and fractured father-son storyline. *Scum*, like *The Loneliness of the Long Distance Runner* before it, helped to create a legacy of angry young teen dramas. Clarke's later film *Made in Britain* (1982) focused on Trevor, a misguided skinhead anti-hero whose violent actions, nihilism and one word manifesto 'Bollerrrrks' provide a handy template for the Shane Meadows classic *This is England* (2006). Stephen Graham's Combo and Tim Roth's Trevor both provided uneasy reflections of Margaret Thatcher's divided Britain. Another skinhead, Coxy (Gary Oldman), featured in Mike Leigh's early film *Meantime* (1983). While the film is an interesting entry in Leigh's canon of work, with some brilliantly nuanced performances, its mood, tone and themes in some ways mirroring those of the later film, *Secrets and Lies* (1996), it feels incomplete but captures that fascinating period between the late 70s and mid-80s perfectly.

At least two of the key actors from the TV and theatrical versions of *Scum* made it into another important working-class teen drama, which was less about physical prisons and more about the identification boxes we place ourselves in — that and cool-looking scooters, sharp suits and parkas.

Quadrophenia (1979) began life as a rock opera, but more importantly, the spark of the idea came when The Who's Pete Townshend read about a young Mod who had committed suicide by throwing himself off Beachy Head. This would have resonated with the aging Townshend. The Who had started life as a custom-made Mod outfit and were part of the original 60s scene. Mods in their original incarnation were all about immaculate handmade Italian-style fashion, well-groomed hair, Motown music and dancehalls. The Mod drug of choice was amphetamine and their mode of transport was the scooter, perfect for inner-city mobility.

Seeking to tap into that wave of nostalgia, Townshend created a double album set-piece. It was a far cry from their earlier, much cooler beat combo efforts, less raw, more overblown and carrying with it all the pretension and pomposity we've come to expect from a mid-70s concept album brought to us by cynical over-paid pop stars. To be fair, there are some interesting moments. *5:15* remains an undoubted classic and *The Real Me* still carries a certain power even today. But the album is bogged down in self-indulgence and an overgrown sense of its own importance, a self-aggrandisement that would take a serious kicking with the coming of punk just a few years later.

When it was suggested that *Quadrophenia* might make an interesting basis for a feature film it was assumed, largely by Townshend, that this would follow a similar path to the one they had pursued with the film adaptation of *Tommy* (1975). In Ken Russell's hands *Tommy* became a bizarre mess of colourful, ostentatious, baked-bean-overflowing, hippy-dippy meaningless bedazzlement. Loved by some and loathed by others, it was a feature-length swaggering arty-farty bit of nonsense seemingly in love with itself. Townshend even went as far as creating a filmic soundtrack to the proposed *Quadrophenia* film, in a similar rock opera style. But any ideas that the film would become a convenient follow-up to *Tommy* were dashed when director Franc Roddam was brought on board.

Roddam took an altogether more down-to-earth approach. Previously, he had worked mainly in documentary. Seminal TV show

The Family, among the first fly-on-the-wall reality shows to hit the airwaves, was one of his early credits. When it came to directing *Quadrophenia* he already had in mind a much more kitchen sink-style approach and was keen to take the idea about as far away from *Tommy* as it was possible to get. First, he needed a cast.

Roddam was intelligent enough to understand that in order to appeal to young modern audiences he would have to place young modern actors within his drama. Though the film was a period piece set around the time of the early 60s Mod and Rocker clashes, it was also a new slice of cinema that could tap into the rebelliousness of the late 70s. Though visually we are treated to immaculate fashions of the day and the look is accurate for the year in which it is set, the production has a very up-to-date punk sensibility. This is helped by its young bunch of protagonists and supporting characters, amongst them Sting and Toyah Willcox, both future stars who were firmly attached to the burgeoning punk scene. Willcox had already appeared alongside Adam Ant in Derek Jarman's lunatic royal knockabout nonsense *Jubilee*. The part of Jimmy Cooper, the disillusioned lead, was originally offered to a post-Sex Pistols John Lydon AKA Johnny Rotten. Roddam had been keen to secure his services — Rotten, king of the punks at that time, would have been a casting coup, but nervous money types were reluctant to provide insurance for the (at least according to *The Sun*) volatile young pop star. So the role went to *Scum*'s Phil Daniels and, like the best casting decisions, it's hard to imagine anyone else straddled across that now-famous scooter.

Roddam also understood that in order for his young cast to act convincingly like an ensemble on screen they would have to bond off screen. In the weeks before filming they were encouraged to go to parties together, they were kitted out in authentic mod regalia, learned to dance and ride scooters and effectively became a gang. The core consisted of Daniels, Willcox, Leslie Ash, Phil Davis, Mark Wingett, Gary Shail, Garry Cooper and Trevor Laird. Other actors included another ex-*Scum* collaborator Ray Winstone as Jimmy's old school friend and token rocker and Kate Williams and Michael Elphick as Jimmy's mother and father.

The more complicated story of the original concept album was jettisoned in favour of a stripped-down narrative. It became a gritty coming-of-age drama, gritty not just in terms of tone but also visually. Though beautifully shot, the grainy look of the film helps to create a ground-down atmosphere of working-class life, the images of claustrophobic offices, tired-looking supermarkets and municipal waste dumps contrast brilliantly with the night clubs, Brighton beach battles and Jimmy's amphetamine-inspired midnight scooter jaunts. The peacock flourishes of Mod life and all that that promises segue into grim-looking slipper baths, pie and mash shops and pokey terrace houses.

Filmed on location, much of the action takes place at night. The opening shots of Jimmy and the gang riding unhindered through the now largely unrecognisable streets of West London with The Who's *The Real Me* pounding over the images provides a fitting start to an adrenaline-rushing feature. Roddam insisted on spraying the roads with water so that under the minimal street lighting they would appear black and shiny, giving the film a much more textured feel.

While the original album focused on the main character's multiple personality issues, hence the title, the film pares this down to a simpler representation of teenage identity angst. Daniels is simply brilliant as Jimmy, switching from rebellious ego-charged party animal to down-at-heel office boy on the world's worst comedown with seemingly effortless joy. His bravado provides a contrast to his deeper-seated insecurity, perhaps never so much as in Jimmy's slightly confused manifesto: 'I don't wanna be like everyone else, that's why I'm a Mod, see?'

There are also moments in the film which hint of more serious mental health issues. In one of the many clashes with his parents, his father proclaims Jimmy to be 'barmy' and 'schizophrenic', detailing how the family might have a history of such problems. But essentially *Quadrophenia*, at least in the hands of Roddam and his young cast, is about disillusionment.

The initial scenes of shagging, pill-popping, wanton vandalism, party gate-crashing and casual violence are all a mere prelude to the main action which takes place when the gang, alongside hundreds of other Mods, arrives for an amphetamine-enhanced Bank Holiday in Brighton. The clashes depicted in the film were based on actual fights between Mods and Rockers in places like Clacton back in the 60s. For extras Roddam used actual Mods and at times the action edged a little too close to reality. There were stories of real police officers being drawn mistakenly into the rioting. The famous Mod march through the seaside town and the accompanying 'We are the Mods, we are the Mods, we are, we are, we are the Mods' would go down in British cinema history and spill out onto thousands of school yards, where it rode the wave of the oncoming Mod revival, spurred on by figureheads like Jam frontman Paul Weller.

But it was other scenes which told us more about Jimmy and his state of mind. In the lead-up to the trip, Jimmy has made no secret of the fact that he is attracted to Steph (Leslie Ash). Steph is already involved with older mod Fenton, who sees Jimmy as nothing more than an annoying upstart. But when Jimmy, in the midst of a riot, has sex with Steph, he believes that she is as besotted with him. It is only when Jimmy is arrested, causing a delayed trip back to London, that things begin to unravel. He is unceremoniously dumped by Steph, who is now seeing Jimmy's one-time best friend, Dave (Mark Wingett). After an angry scuffle, he rides off home only to find he's been slung out on to the streets. After a damp night in his dad's allotment shed, he manages to make things worse when, in a crash involving a post van, his beloved scooter is destroyed.

Taking the train to Brighton, with a pocket full of blues and the last of his wages, Jimmy goes in search of the one thing which still makes sense, the pinnacle of all his Mod dreams — the Ace Face. The Face, played by a young bleached-blond Sting (real name Gordon Sumner) is, at least in Jimmy's eyes, the epitome of all things cool, the Mod Everest, the unreachable attainment of everything worth living for. Jimmy has grown to believe that he somehow shares an affinity with The Face, due to being arrested and going to court on the same day. But like his mistaken beliefs about Steph's intentions, his dreams are dashed when he learns that Ace is no more than a bossed-about bellboy in one of Brighton's posh sea-front hotels. In a moment of realisation, he steals the gleaming silver GS scooter belonging to his ex-hero and rides it out along the vertigo-inducing cliff tops, the seagulls circling above like vultures over carrion. In a final act of defiance, Jimmy sends the scooter over the cliffs to crash against the rocky beach below. It is one of the most misunderstood moments in screen history, many still believing that Jimmy commits suicide — he does not. The death we witness is merely the end of his religious-like devotion to all things Mod. In fact, we see the end of the story at the beginning of the film when Jimmy walks away from the cliff tops into the camera. Just what he is walking back to is unclear. Though his realisation is perhaps overdue, we also hope that Jimmy is not 'growing up' in the traditional sense. But we are still left with a central question: will his realisation lead to a deeper understanding of who he is or will he lose sight of that altogether and become his father or something else?

The film remains a genuine classic, and unlike most classics it does seem to transcend the generations. There are several reasons, I believe, why the film still resonates with mixed audiences even today. Firstly, the look of the film in terms of the presentation of Mod culture is still very appealing. Mod, unlike many sub-cultures, still holds much fascination for younger people. There's no getting around the fact that this is a good-looking film. Secondly, while this is, by today's standards, a period piece, it still feels fresh, partly because the Mod image is so resolutely appreciated but partly because what the film is actually about — youth and disillusionment — is so universal. *Quadrophenia* has much more in common with John Badham's *Saturday Night Fever* (1977) than it does with, say, *Room at the Top*. Though *Saturday Night Fever* is set in the 70s and is centred around the New York disco scene, its content is remarkably similar. Jimmy may have seen Tony as an exotic foreigner, but their journeys seem to run in parallel. Thirdly, Roddam as director plays with our expectations, overturning certain stereotypical tropes. For instance, the female characters are largely in charge in *Quadrophenia*. Steph certainly calls the shots when it comes to both Jimmy and Pete, and it is clear that Jimmy's mother runs the household. Roddam gives us nudity, but in a turnabout of usual standards, it is only ever male nudity. Lastly, the soundtrack to *Quadrophenia* is superb, not so much The Who's contributions, which are okay, but the string of 60s classics which accompany the action and include artists like The Chiffons, The Ronnettes, The Crystals and Booker T and the MGs. Like the music, *Quadrophenia* is both memorable and stylish, while it deals with class issues, it also rises above them. *Quadrophenia* is a well-made, beautifully-presented teen angst drama whose achingly cool surface can be peeled back to reveal a fundamental truth about being and existence. As the posters once screamed, 'IT'S A WAY OF LIFE'.

12: Choose Life

It's shite being Scottish! We're the lowest of the low. The scum of the fucking Earth! The most wretched, miserable, servile, pathetic trash that was ever shat into civilization. Some hate the English. I don't. They're just wankers. We, on the other hand, are colonized by wankers. Can't even find a decent culture to be colonized by. We're ruled by effete assholes. It's a shite state of affairs to be in, Tommy, and all the fresh air in the world won't make any fucking difference.

Trainspotting (1996)

1982 brought the UK the Falklands War, *E.T.*, the World Cup and a brand-new television channel. In these days of streaming and an endless supply of cheap twenty-four-hour TV output, it's difficult to either remember or imagine, if you weren't there, the landscape of British television before the introduction of Channel 4. The BBC, for all its faults and virtues, began delivering its TV presentations in 1936. It was limited in its content and distribution and, between 1939 and 1945, its broadcasts were shelved due to the Second World War. Its radio output largely proved more popular than its televisual content until the coronation of Queen Elizabeth II in 1952, when sales of television sets boomed. The BBC remained unchallenged until the appearance of ITV in 1954. There was the introduction of BBC2 in 1969, and colour presentations, but UK television remained a largely-unchanged three-channel affair until Channel 4 crashed onto our screens in the autumn of 1982.

While some of the shows from its first day of broadcasting have been consigned to the bargain bin of history, such as *The Body Show*, *The People's Court* and the god-awful *Paul Hogan Show*, much of what remains from its inaugural evening demonstrates just how determined the channel was to shake up the world of television. *Brookside*, for instance, which aired on the channel's prime time slot, ran for twenty-one years and forced the world of soap opera to up its game considerably with its red-top-baiting story lines which included lesbian affairs, incest, murder and domestic abuse. There was also the first-ever episode of *The Comic Strip Presents*, featuring a raft of performers and writers torn from the stages of a burgeoning new comedy scene. For most viewers it would be the first time they had clapped eyes on the likes of Dawn French, Jennifer Saunders, Rik Mayall, Ade Edmondson and Nigel Planer. *Walter* was also aired, a Stephen Frears made-for-TV film starring a young Ian McKellen struggling with learning difficulties. The channel chose to close its first day of operation by showing the documentary *In the Pink*, which not only showreeled the work of a feminist cabaret group but also cemented the channel's agenda, which was to provide an alternative to existing channels and to create programming for minority groups.

To some, though, the new broadcaster would be branded as a left-leaning troublemaker. It's difficult to overstate just how much Channel 4, particularly in its initial years as a broadcaster, changed the way people saw television. Whilst previously viewers may have thought of BBC2 as the arts broadcaster, with more intellectual leanings that its sister channel BBC1, BBC2 had often felt more class-based and largely appealed to older licence payers. Channel 4 was fresher and actively engaged with a younger demographic; it was unmistakably anti-establishment (or about as anti-establishment as a legal broadcaster could be). Its content divided people. In its first few years it would agitate the mainstream media and send the *Daily Mail* into frothing fits of front page rage with its late-night red triangle films, cutting-edge drama, risqué comedy and unabashed obscenity. But to younger audiences (particularly teenagers such as myself at the time) the channel couldn't have come at a more opportune moment.

The UK was mired in the prospect of another five years of Tory rule. Thatcher, still basking in her Falklands War victory, had seemingly kicked the chair from beneath the feet of a depressed-looking Labour Party, unemployment was monumentally high and the prospect of a nuclear conflict felt more likely with each passing month. Channel 4's output, including *The Tube*, *Saturday Night Live*, *Max Headroom* and show runners like *Brookside*, provided a welcome escape from the BBC's stuffiness and the populist prime time fluff of ITV. It was a mixed bag of hard-hitting, raunchy, controversial, funny and bizarre. Channel 4 was the cool kid at the party.

It wasn't just the channel's radical approach that was appealing, it was also its randomness. Animated efforts like the strangely surreal *Murun Buchstansangur*, about an odd creature who lived under the sink, helped galvanise the broadcaster's off-kilter viewpoint. There was also the now largely forgotten *Gunston's Australia* which featured a fake on-the-scene reporter, out to poke fun at unsuspecting celebrities, in a show which predated *Borat*, *Dennis Pennis* and *Jonathan Pie* by a good many years. The channel was also unafraid to revisit the past. I remember being enthralled by repeats of old shows like *Budgie*, starring Adam Faith, or *The Munsters*, or a complete run of Rod Serling's amazing series *The Twilight Zone*. Later, Jonathan Ross brought a more American-style approach to the chat show with *The Last Resort* and also opened up the world of cult cinema, perhaps for the first time on television, with *The Incredibly Strange Film Show*. Channel 4 was the original home for Vic Reeves and Bob Mortimer, Avid Merrion (AKA Leigh Francis), Sacha Baron Cohen and Ricky Gervais. It also brought black sitcoms like *No Problem* and, much more successfully, *Desmond's* to a large UK audience for the first time.

An important aspect of Channel 4 was its film production company, which later came to be known as Film Four. Over the years, it made and funded a large number of features produced in the UK and all over the world. In recent times, it has supported Ben Wheatley features like *A Field in England*, *High Rise* and *Free Fire*, powerful work such as Paddy Considine's *Tyrannosaur* and critically-acclaimed pieces *Shame*, *Wuthering Heights* and *Berberian Sound Studio*. In its history it has provided exposure to the work of key film-makers and has played an important role in the promotion of cutting-edge British film.

Its impressive CV includes *Prick up Your Ears*, *My Beautiful Laundrette*, *Local Hero*, *Letter to Brezhnev*, *Mona Lisa*, *A Room with a View*, *The Company of Wolves*, *The Crying Game*, *Life is Sweet* and a strangely hypnotic, Brit-pop-charged knockabout comedy about heroin and cot death...

Trainspotting (1996) began life as the debut novel of Irvine Welsh. From 1991, Leith-born Welsh had been writing short stories which were published in places like *DOG*, the *West Coast Magazine* and *New Writing Scotland*. Some of these stories eventually went on to form parts of *Trainspotting*. The original novel is more akin to a collection of short episodes than a coherent well-structured narrative, and its main protagonist, Renton, is a harder, less redeemable character than the fairly affable one presented by Ewan McGregor in the film adaptation. The book offers a non-socialist glimpse into the lives of a Scottish working class or under-class. Renton is the embodiment of scepticism, a ragged-arse, two-fingered salute to do-gooding social workers and therapists who exist within a system which cannot deal with the fact that many choose to live beyond the outskirts of its hypocritical control.

> Ah choose no tae choose life. If the cunts cannae handle
> that, it's thair fuckin problem.

Written in authentically thick Leithian dialect, it's a beautiful and brutal paean to the outsider. It was violent, messy, shocking and exceedingly popular. Released at a time when Edinburgh was often cited as being the HIV capital of Europe, it delved uncomfortably into the city's heroin problem, highlighting the double standards of society and what happens when you concentrate on the symptoms whilst ignoring the disease. Welsh's carefully-crafted raw energy seemed to tap into the heart of 90s subculture. It was both critically well-received and rejected by the establishment. Its prospects of being shortlisted for the Booker Prize were apparently dashed after the novel had 'offended the sensibilities' of two of the judges. Despite this, it was adapted initially into a touring stage play and soon a proposed film adaptation was touted.

Danny Boyle, who went on to make *The Beach*, *28 Days Later*, *Sunshine* and *Slumdog Millionaire*, in the mid-90s only had one previous film credit as director. *Shallow Grave* (1994) was a neat little thriller, violent, funny, adept and skilfully handled. It tapped into ideas previously worked over in films like *The Treasure of the Sierra Madre* and *Trespass*, but placed the film's themes of greed, mistrust and paranoia within the city of Edinburgh, centring on three impossibly smug flatmates played by Ewan McGregor, Kerry Fox and Christopher Ecclestone. When they agree to rent out their spare room to a stranger (Keith Allen) after humiliating a string of other would-be tenants, they are shocked when they discover their new housemate is dead the next morning. Simply reporting the body to the police is put on hold when the three realise that their late tenant also has in his possession a large sum of money. From here on in the film becomes a mad and murderous triangle of deceit and criminality. Ecclestone steals the show as the calculating and swiftly-emerging psychotic David. The film won a host of awards and quickly launched Boyle as a serious prospect when it came to British film-making.

When it came to adapting *Trainspotting*, it was clear that a film version would require an alternative approach in bringing some kind of universal story to life. Working closely with screenwriter John Hodge, Boyle was able to strip away much of the denseness of the text, fashioning many of the stories from the book into a workable and more cinematic offering. While the novel is unrelentingly real and naturalistic in its delivery, Boyle's film is one of much less literal interpretation, seeding the reality of heroin addiction, poverty and violence with brilliantly-realised symbolic imagery. Take one of its most famous scenes for instance, where Renton, who has decided to quit heroin again, takes one more hit before going cold turkey. The hit he takes, out of necessity, comes in the form of two suppositories, but a bout of nuclear-powered diarrhoea causes him to lose his vital medication when he is forced to unload his exploding bowels in the worst public convenience in Scotland. Realising too late, Renton is compelled to stick his arm into the blocked toilet bowl to reclaim his prize. It's a stomach-churning scene. Renton gags and spits as his hand sinks deeper into God knows what, the contents of the swilling porcelain slopping onto the already-filthy floor, and we begin to understand that this is the lowest a man can go. Then the scene takes on a more surreal edge. In desperation Renton sinks his other hand into the bowl then his head and pretty soon his entire body squirms impossibly into the toilet and disappears. We cut to Renton inside not a cramped sewer pipe, but a beautiful blue lagoon. He floats happily thorough the dreamlike waters before finding his lost suppositories and swimming back up through the toilet and into reality once again. It's a perfectly-rendered moment which deals at cinematic and symbolic levels with Welsh's point from the novel, which is that an addict will crawl through shit if there's a hit at the end of it. There are many such moments in the film. While the novel might have been a ground-breaking piece of literature, the film is an innovative and evocative piece of cinema. At one point, an overdosing Renton sinks into and through the floor, in another he jumps from an outside wall and when he lands he is inside his dealer's flat, and during his cold turkey Boyle treats us to a nightmarish montage of TV game shows, surreal imagery and guilt-laden hallucinations.

Trainspotting is an optical feast, but for all of its visual flourishes, at its heart is a strong story about addiction in all of its forms, whether that be heroin, gambling, television, capitalism, prescription drugs or alcohol. It never flinches in delivering some of the same uncomfortable truths to be found in Welsh's original novel. Infant mortality, AIDS, criminality and under-age sex all lurk close to the film's surface-level presentation of knockabout humour, violence and unlikely friendships. Boyle was able to assemble an excellent cast of young actors who believably brought to life the kind of reprobate outlaws that were presented within the text. These included Renton (Ewan McGregor), the protagonist and ostensibly the most relatable character; Sick Boy (Jonny Lee Miller), a cold James Bond obsessive and occasional pimp; Tommy (Kevin McKidd), a likeable football fan and until his eventual demise from AIDS, often the most upbeat of the gang; Spud (Ewen Bremner), a gormless soul whose heart is in the right place; and thug Begbie (Robert Carlyle).

Though each character is well-formed and under the direction of Boyle they become contrasting yet essential pieces in the film's cleverly strung-together narrative, Robert Carlyle's portrayal of Begbie, an uncouth foul-mouthed sociopath, is the most engaging. In some ways Begbie represents the deep-seated hypocrisy that poisons any attempt to begin to deal with a problem like heroin addiction. He looks down on addicts while ignoring his own life-destroying dependencies on gambling and alcohol, and his supposed hatred of smack only stretches as far as when he is presented with a one-time opportunity to make a life-changing sum of money from an ill-advised drug deal.

In the famous climax of the film, the gang — Begbie, Renton, Sick Boy and Spud — languish in a cheap hotel room. Each character is sleeping off a heavy session. Begbie clings onto a bag full of drug deal money, in which they all have a share. Renton, though, is not sleeping. In a moment of madness, he skilfully prises the bag from Begbie's unconscious hands and escapes, while reticent Spud looks on. Out of context, there is still tension to be gained from the scene but placed quickly after the last section of the film, in which we've just seen a nervous and drunken Begbie glass a man in the face and threaten a whole pub with his knife, the tension becomes unbearable. One slip and Renton will almost certainly wind up dead. It's also in the former scene that Carlyle really illustrates his incredible ability to inhabit an oddity like Begbie. Not only does he demonstrate the character's uncontrolled rage, highlighting the danger he poses to his enemies and especially his so-called friends, he also, just moments later, shows us the vulnerable side of his personality when he asks a shaking Sick Boy to light his cigarette for him. It's here we see Begbie for who he really is, an out-of-his-depth schoolyard bully failing to find his place in the world. His outward confidence, bluster and high-volume outrage do little to hide the fact that he's essentially lost.

Trainspotting is an entertaining feature which never lets up in pace or tension, from the opening scenes of Renton being chased by security guards against the pounding backbeat of Iggy Pop's *Lust for Life*, to the illusory nature of the overdose sequence, replete with its ironic *Perfect Day* Lou Reed soundscape. It's a film which partly seems to yearn for the past and is in some respects an important part of the future. But it was also very much a part of the present. Aside from old school musical nods to the 70s and 80s, the film embedded itself exactly where it needed to be, its place in the 'now' cemented not just by its Brit Pop credentials but also by its fresh ideas and vitality. This was Boyle at his creative peak. Though the sequel, *T2 Trainspotting*, was popular and it brought in more elements from the original book, the project felt a little forced, as though stuck in its own nostalgia, and it never really reached the heights or matched the cinematic flair of its predecessor. *Trainspotting* had much to say even though essentially it had nothing to say, it was political because it was so apolitical. Perhaps the film is best summed up by its own opening anti-manifesto.

> Choose rotting away at the end of it all, pishing away your last in a miserable home nothing more than an embarrassment to the selfish, fucked-up brats you have spawned to replace yourself. Choose your future. Choose life.

13: Life is Bitter Sweet

*Was I bored? No, I wasn't fuckin' bored. I'm never bored. That's
the trouble with everybody — you're all so bored. You've 'ad
nature explained to you, and you're bored with it. You've 'ad the
living body explained to you, and you're bored with it. You've 'ad
the universe explained to you, and you're bored with it.*

Naked (1993)

There's a lovely moment in the 1996 film *Secrets and Lies*. A montage of
shots which all happen within the confines of Maurice Purley's
photographic studio plays out before us, suggesting just how successful
he is in terms of customer turn-out and also how good he is at his chosen
profession. It gives us a handy snapshot of his character — a friendly
and generous, good-natured human being. But more interesting are the
actors playing the customers in that scene. Those eagle-eyed enough will
recognise amongst their number Alison Steadman, Liz Smith, Peter
Wight and Anthony O'Donnell — all have appeared previously in plays
or films by the same director, including *Nuts in May*, *Life is Sweet*, *Naked*
and *Hard Labour*. They provide neat little cameos, brief blink-of-an-eye
moments, but although their appearances are fleeting their presence
seems to indicate a fondness and genuine willingness to be attached to
the work of one man and his latest project. That man is Mike Leigh.

Son of a doctor, Mike Leigh was educated at Salford Grammar School
before gaining a scholarship to the Royal Academy for Dramatic Art in
1960. He would also spend time at Camberwell School of Arts and
Crafts, Central School of Art and Design, and London Film School. By
1965 he was beginning to devise his own stage plays and this culminated
in a piece called *Bleak Moments*, which he adapted into his first feature
film.

The simple narrative, almost non-narrative, of *Bleak Moments* (1971)
seems to play out on the edges. Like the socially awkward characters who
inhabit the film, the plot is hesitant, insecure and at odds with itself and
the rest of the world. And yet it's fascinating because of that. Anne Raitt
as introverted, lonely secretary, Sylvia, seems to hover at the periphery of
day-to-day machinations, no more engaged with the social complexities
of office life or leisure activities than her mentally disabled sister, who she
spends much of her time looking after. Her appearance, widow-like and
perfunctory as if she were a passion-free Morticia Addams, punctuates
her inability to chime with any sense of joy. Thick black eye make-up gives

131

her face a mask-like countenance, unbroken, unchanging — a soul incapable or undesirous of reaching beyond monotony. She shares her bleak moments with a host of equally unremarkable personalities, all seemingly lost in their own. Her only female companion is work colleague Pat, and their friendship is sparse at best. Also entering her life at various times are Norman, a shy guitar-strumming hippy, and Peter, her boyfriend, largely in name only, their relationship moving from desultory to dejected. There is a hollowness to Sylvia, bought about brilliantly by Raitt. Her performance seems to mirror that of Sylvia Kay as Janette in *Wake in Fright*, an Australian feature released the same year. Both characters exude emptiness as though there is literally nothing left. But while Janette tragically uses alcohol intoxication and casual sex as a desperate form of reaching out, Sylvia cannot seem to break through on any level. The quiet discomfort that even light conversation causes highlights a sense of worthlessness for which even Janette in her ragged and inebriated state might feel sympathy.

After *Bleak Moments* Leigh moved away from feature films and did not return properly to the cinema till 1988 with his film *High Hopes*, although *Meantime* (1983) received a limited theatrical release. Between 1971 and 1988 he developed nine plays for television, his first being the sombre *Hard Labour* which was followed by *The Kiss of Death*, both set in the North West of England, but most of his work tended to be set around the 'suburban south'.

Nuts in May (1976), which focused on self-righteous and decidedly odd campers, Candice Marie and Keith Pratt, was the fifth of Leigh's television plays, and forty-two years after its first transmission it has lost none of its charm, wit and originality. There's no doubt its DNA runs through the veins of Ben Wheatley's excellent 2012 film *Sightseers*.

This well-placed comedy mixed with its fluctuating levels of eccentricity make for an entertaining and heady tale of countryside clashes, and as with *Bleak Moments* there is a range of characters who fail on any level to communicate effectively. Keith's initial low-level pedantry, for instance, and his petty insistence on obeying the holiday rules at all costs, regardless of whether any outsiders are aware of his unshifting manifesto, can only ever lead to a climax of unsettling public displays of violence, with Keith descending into a log-swinging psychotic tantrum.

Pratt (Roger Sloman) and his passively aggressive wife Candice Marie (Alison Steadman), make for excellent exhibits in what would become

Leigh's growing menagerie of 'middle-class monsters'. While they may not be monsters in the truly malevolent sense, no one in their right mind would want to shoot the breeze with them over a bowl of organic muesli and unhomogenized milk, and it's clear the title of the play refers not to the couple's choice of healthy snacks but to the couple themselves. Their self-righteousness and borderline insanity comes quickly to the surface when they come up against less middle-class characters, who fail to share their belief that a holiday is not to be enjoyed but to be endured. They clash awkwardly at first with Ray (Anthony O'Donnell), a down-to-earth PE teacher who dares to play his radio, shattering the natural silence that Keith and Candice Marie have come to expect. Though they try to break bread later, it is clear their own dogmatic approach to existence will always get in the way of actual human contact. But while relations may become strained with Ray, particularly when they cajole him unwillingly into a socially embarrassing sing-song-come-lecture, things turn ballistic when Finger (Stephen Bill) and Honky (Sheila Kelley), complete with football, motorbike and distinct lack of understanding for the Country Code, career onto the hallowed campsite, farting, shouting and shagging their way into the delicate ecosystem of the Pratts.

Brummie plasterer Finger, an uncouth but harmless enough young reprobate, accompanied by his inappropriately attired girlfriend Honky, all leather jacket and Suzi Quatro sequined platforms, provide an immediate challenge to Candice Marie and especially to Keith. The new arrivals with their working-class brand of low-level hedonism and the common touch provide a stark contrast to the Pratts' own idea of holiday heaven, namely a strict regime of minutely planned excursions and meal times, where a 'treat' comes in the form of a handful of raw mushrooms. The final straw, for Keith at least, comes when Finger attempts to start a fire. In the absence of the camp's manager, Keith launches into a strongly worded and ultimately violent outburst concerning basic health and safety regulations. But as Keith devolves into a snivelling, angry wreck, it is arguable whether his wrath has been brought on purely by a breaking of the rules or whether there is also a sense of betrayal on the part of Ray, who has turned his back on the Pratts' pathetic attempt to befriend him in order to get drunk with Honky and Finger. Aside from this betrayal, Keith's previous trust in authority is brought into question towards the end of the film, when not only is he let down by the camp's owner but he is also treated like a criminal by a local copper who berates him for having a bald tyre.

While it is not perhaps the absolute focus of *Nuts in May*, the clashes between the classes are interesting. The obvious cultural differences and work/life experiences of the Pratts when compared to Finger and Honky are clear, not least in the conversations that the two couples have about their current employment. While Finger and Honky seem fairly ambivalent about their jobs, neither hating them nor loving them, Keith and Candice Marie exude a sense of self-importance about their livelihoods, as though their low-level middle-class occupations give them a greater entitlement to holidays and happiness. Ray, who is drifting towards the more traditionally middle-class profession of teaching, seems, at least on a social level, more at ease with working-class sensibility. When the Pratts try to force him into singing along with a rendition of one of their hopeless self-indulgent musical numbers, it ends in an awkward and embarrassing failure. Yet he sings along loudly to a traditional working-class musical number, *She Was Poor But She Was Honest*, with Finger and Honky when the three stagger home drunkenly from the pub.

Though *Nuts in May* is hilarious in places, the tragedy of the situation seems to lie, as in *Bleak Moments*, with the central characters' absolute inability to fit in or connect with any level of society. The Pratts appear to drift from one social context to another with increasingly poor results. They are sneered at by tradesmen, ripped off by farmers, treated as oddities by other holidaymakers and mistrusted by the authorities such as the campsite owner and local constabulary. And yet they never question their motives or their daily failures to communicate or engage with other human beings. It is their absolute class-bound certainty that the world must fit around their needs and not the other way around that places the Pratts at odds with day-to-day life and its citizens. Their stubbornness is rammed home in the final moments when we watch a determined Keith march into the twilight, armed only with a shovel and a toilet roll.

Leigh followed *Nuts in May* with another iconic slice of 70s television, which has probably become his most fondly-remembered piece of work. *Abigail's Party*, originally a stage play, was abridged and adapted for the BBCs *Play for Today* in 1977. Strangely, as she is throwing a party at home next door, the eponymous Abigail is never seen, being the fifteen-year-old daughter of divorcée neighbour Sue. The action takes place in the home of overbearing Beverly, brilliantly played by Alison Steadman, who is throwing what she believes to be a sophisticated soirée in the heart of suburban Romford. Present at this social gathering are the downtrodden Laurence (Beverly's husband), mousy neighbour Sue and newly moved in to the street couple Tony and Angela. What transpires is an evening of misplaced flirting, breakdowns in communication and awkward public displays of suburbanite frustration which pour out as freely as the cheap Beaujolais. Whilst its look and sound — trimphones, MFI furniture, polyester frocks and Demis Roussos — sets this up as a period piece (some of its subsequent adaptations can lean heavily towards nostalgia), much of what it has to say, particularly its observations about aspirational lower-middle-class hopes, still rings true. By the time we have reached the chaotic climax, where the comedy is snatched away and we are left with a typical flash of Leigh's dark shading, leaving Beverly's husband in cardiac arrest on the well-hoovered carpet, we have been party to all the obsessions, prejudices, pettiness and fears of a collection of aspirational characters who don't seem to know what they are aspiring to or why.

By the time Leigh returned to film-making in 1988, almost two decades after *Bleak Moments*, he had begun to develop a process enabling him to translate concepts onto the screen more effectively. Very often there was no initial script, Leigh often bringing nothing more than notions or themes to the table. Instead the actors would workshop ideas or moments until characters and situations would present themselves more naturally, and while Leigh is his own film-maker, similar techniques have also been employed by Ken Loach and Shane Meadows. Critics have occasionally accused him of creating grotesques or caricatures instead of rounded characters and there is some evidence of this: Sally Hawkins as Poppy, for instance, in Leigh's 2008 film *Happy-Go-Lucky* can sometimes come across as a sort of groundless unrelatable oddity. But perhaps these criticisms are only aimed at this particular director *because* he is British and there is a certain predisposed expectation about authenticity and social realism when it comes to the UK film industry. But aren't many Hollywood features or French rom-coms, for instance, just as brimming with un-relatable oddities?

Despite these arguments there are numerous examples where Leigh has presented us with breathtaking cinematic delights of unquestionable quality, but it is his ability to bring us pockets of life which play with comic nuance and more serious concerns that really cement him as being one the UK's most innovative film-makers. There is something beautifully unique about a Mike Leigh film. While his work can be compared favourably to other directors of his generation, there is an off-kilterness to his output which places his films beyond the remit of more formulaic productions. Though there is certainly a 'kitchen sink' element to many of his films, and a genuine grittiness, particularly in the case of *Vera Drake*, there is also a slight otherworldliness present in his work. Even when we are confronted with shocking, violent or emotionally challenging material, we never quite forget we are viewing a theatrical presentation. Though there are hints of what we might call social realism, it feels heightened. The rawness is packaged so artfully that we accept the artifice without ever losing interest in the characters or their lives.

His filmography to date includes *Career Girls* (1997), *Topsy Turvy* (1999), *All or Nothing* (2002), *Vera Drake* (2004), *Happy-Go-Lucky* (2008), *Another Year* (2010), *Mr Turner* (2014), and, as this book is being written, his latest work, *Peterloo*, based on the Peterloo Massacre, is about to hit the cinemas. For many, myself included, his short run of films from 1990 to 1996 remains his most satisfying and challenging period. And while this is not to downgrade his other efforts, there is something very Mike Leigh about those three particular Mike Leigh films.

Life is Sweet (1990) focuses on the ups and downs of a North London working-class family headed up by the innuendo-charged matriarch, Wendy (Alison Steadman). Wendy is married to Andy (Jim Broadbent), an affable, yet somewhat unfulfilled senior chef, and is mother to twenty-two-year-old twin girls. The drama rolls out over a number of balmy summer weeks, the heat only adding to the sense of closed-in family home life. We become party to the various machinations which surround and affect the tight domestic unit and are introduced to other non-family members who enter and exit in a series of comic and tragic episodes. Though we are presented with Leigh's customary cast of contrasting players, the action is filmed in a way which never leads us to side with any one character. The camera moves unselectively from one person to the next, as if it is asking us to accept each state of mind and separate position of its featured personas. As in most of Leigh's films, with *Life is Sweet* we are given not so much a plot with a clear through line, as a collection of carefully captured incidents. Within this, members of the family and their viewpoints are explored and laid bare. Nicola, for instance, played by a young, squeaky-voiced Jane Horrocks, presents not just a challenging personality for her family and the audience, but also for herself. A joyless chain-smoking, simmering martyr to her own pessimism, she stalks the house, which she never leaves, decked out in a custom-made 'Bollocks to the Poll Tax' T-shirt and John Lennon specs. She is as angry and cynical as she is ineffective: 'I am political. Shut the door.'

Her twin Natalie, played by a pre-*Outnumbered* Claire Skinner, seems more at home with family life, more at ease with both her parents, and she takes to the ordinary concerns of everyday existence, including work and money and planning for the future, with none of the fear and mistrust of her scathingly political sibling. And yet Natalie is in many ways more radical than Nicola can ever dare to be. Natalie rejects gender stereotypes, both in her tomboyish appearance and choice of profession — a plumber's mate. 'I put my hand down toilets and on a good day I might get bit by a rat.' And her unspoken form of radicalism only underlines her ability to act, in the face of Nicola's inaction. For all her talk, her hissed remarks about being a feminist, Nicola's loud apathy becomes apparent when juxtaposed with Natalie's quiet working-class rebellion.

The girls' mother Wendy, a toddlers' dance instructor, appears to be the emotional rock at the heart of the family, which is not to say that she doesn't struggle with the disquiet which bubbles away below the surface, particularly when it comes to her troubled daughter Nicola. And when Andy decides to buy a dilapidated old van from dodgy Patsy (Stephen Rea), with a view to cleaning it up for a proposed fast food business, Wendy is both supportive and naturally sceptical. She is also the secret crush of Aubrey (Timothy Spall), an idiotic, pudgy loser decked in sub-Timmy Mallett apparel. He's a ludicrously deluded family acquaintance whose phony business acumen and misplaced confidence lead to him opening a disastrous French-themed restaurant. When his ill-prepared venture goes for a burton on the opening night, Aubrey, a bloated bag of broken dreams, gets drunk and makes an awkward pass at Wendy, who has agreed to waitress for him when his paid member of staff goes AWOL. It's a cringe-making scene of utter catastrophe, a rejected Aubrey clumsily waddling around the restaurant, graceless, stripped to his pants, throwing over tables and ripping pictures from the walls before passing out on the floor with the knocked-over candlesticks and crumpled white tablecloths. It's a quintessential slice of Mike Leigh uneasiness which follows humour with bitterness.

Yet despite the film's voyeuristic style, it is without malice or judgement, and it steers away from stereotyped depictions of a suburban working class, instead presenting us with a moving presentation of deep familial bonds. The film's heart is never worn as clearly on its sleeve as in the last half of the story. A stubbornly vitriolic Nicola is finally challenged by Wendy, in a moving moment which sees her confront her daughter's previously unspoken-of bulimia. We learn that Nicola was once admitted to hospital after nearly starving to death. It's a genuinely touching vignette, but one that never feels forced or contrived.

Despite some of its gloomier revelations, *Life is Sweet* remains one of Leigh's lighter outings, and its summertime setting, complete with sun-streaked windows, birdsong and long daylight hours, which are highlighted by the white and floral walls of the family house, only act as a sharp contrast to the director's next venture.

Naked (1993) presents us with an altogether darker chapter in Leigh's oeuvre, both figuratively and literally. Gone are the sunlit yards and neatly-trimmed lawns of the suburban housing estate of *Life is Sweet*, instead we are introduced to a world of shadowy curtain-drawn living rooms, dingy-looking kitchenettes and stark, sterile office blocks which line the grimy back streets of East London. During the two-hour-plus feature Leigh takes us on a gloomy tour of the city's late-night locales where its beleaguered inhabitants become no more than animated shadow puppets, silhouetted against a backdrop of harshly-lit off licenses, faltering neon signs and grim twenty-four hour garages.

The film begins with Johnny (David Thewlis), a scruffy cigarette chugging misanthrope, fleeing his home city of Manchester after a rough sexual encounter with a woman turns into actual rape. Leigh doesn't just suggest this, we are shown the simple and barbaric act in all its pervasive back-alley misery. Fearing violent retribution from the girl's family, he escapes the city in a stolen car and heads out to London, in search of ex-girlfriend Louise.

The sparse-looking credits play out over Johnny's dark journey into the soul, visually referencing Janet Leigh's lonely car ride in Hitchcock's *Psycho*. There are other scenes which could also have been lifted from earlier thriller or horror films. Later, for example, when Johnny meets a young homeless girl, they find themselves wandering beneath an underpass, discussing the nature of hell and the devil. Filmed at a low angle from a distance, it captures German Expressionist-like shadows, the dark arches above them becoming foreboding and unnatural. The bleak *mise-en-scène*, with its stray dogs and dwindling fire in the background, also seems to create the post-apocalyptic landscape which conspiracy theorist Johnny believes is just around the corner.

Upon arriving at Louise's house, he discovers that she is at work. He is invited in though by Sophie (Katrin Cartlidge), Louise's perpetually-stoned housemate, a wraith-like goth, all Siouxsie Sioux fishnets and clueless desperation. The two strangers strike up an odd conversation and it is here that we are allowed to experience Johnny in full flow for the first time. He is, despite obvious psychological personality flaws, a fascinating creation, an intelligent and erudite pessimist and comedian. A dark preacher, his words dancing skilfully between crude sexual innuendo and profoundly unsettling Manc-twinged philosophies and Bible-thumping revelations. Both motor-mouthed and thoughtful, well-read and brutal, Johnny is a ragged contradiction, like Alex from *A Clockwork Orange* he is both wildly charismatic and deeply repellent.

After an altercation involving Sophie and the returned Louise (Lesley Sharp), Johnny finds himself wandering the streets in a self-imposed exile, a manky odyssey of dimly-lit non-adventures where he encounters homeless Archie, an angry and uncommunicative Scot (played by Ewen Bremner in his pre-Spud from *Trainspotting* days), a quiet ghost-like girl in a café (Gina McKee), a drunk woman who he at first seduces then cruelly spurns, and Brian, an embittered and self-important security guard. It is during this last meeting that Leigh fully explores Johnny's delusional or (depending on your view on conspiracy theories or the Book of Revelations) perfectly rational views about the world and its future, or rather, lack of it.

> I'm not talking about astrology. I'm talking about astronomy. They are gonna line up in the fixed signs of Aquarius, Leo, Taurus and Scorpio, which just happen to correspond to the four beasts of the Apocalypse, as mentioned in the Book of Daniel. Another fuckin' fact! D'you want me to go on? The end of the world is nigh, Bri. The game is up!

Johnny's spiky attitude and absence of any natural social grace winds up with him being beaten up, first by an impatient poster-flyer and then by a random group of thugs.

Meanwhile, Sophie and Louise are terrorised by a violent predator known as both Jeremy and Sebastian. He masquerades as their landlord, sexually assaults Sophie and is eventually fought off at knife point. If

Johnny is somewhat of a moral chasm, a corrupted underclass distortion, then Jeremy/Sebastian (Greg Cruttwell) is the embodiment of evil, the Satan of injured Johnny's concussed hallucinations. He's a none-too-subtle metaphor for big city disdain, a giggling monied-up wanker of the worst pre-millennial persuasion.

Towards the climax there is a brief moment of tenderness when Sophie and Johnny (bleeding and cradled in her arms) mouth the words to an old Mancunian song, but this touching scene is soon over and the nihilistic film ends with a limping Johnny heading once more out on to the unforgiving streets.

Whereas *Life is Sweet* appears to be an intimate portrait of family, with tender moments and funny episodes tempered with some darker content, *Naked* provides us with an almost opposite approach where a fleeting glimpse of tenderness can only ever get lost in the uneasy pattern of angry, depressing, bleak twists and turns. Its action is made even more urgent and disturbing by the beautifully chaotic Andrew Dickson score. There is no family at the heart of this piece, it is the absence of family or its equivalent which is most telling. It's a difficult film to watch. Yet *Naked* does (or should) stand as being Mike Leigh's true masterpiece, not despite these negative qualities but because of them.

In terms of reaching a rather more commercial audience, Leigh was probably on safer ground with *Secrets and Lies*. This is not to say that it is not a brave and sometimes challenging piece of work, because it is, but with this film the director again places a family (albeit a highly dysfunctional one) at its centre. Released the same year as *Trainspotting*, *Secrets and Lies* is a story about human frailty and strength, and life's unspoken narratives. For the most part it's a quiet film, full of understated conversations, muted snatched moments lost in the achingly ordinary wall-to-wall domesticity. But the secrets of the title bubble impatiently to the surface and there are several key scenes where the raging sub-text batters itself into the lives of a collection of carefully-formed characters. In one such moment, white Cynthia (Brenda Blethyn) is confronted for the first time with an adult black daughter that she gave away at birth. Though the discussion takes place on the phone, and Blethyn is emoting to a plastic receiver, it's an incredible piece of acting, as we witness an already fairly fractured character break down into a tear-stained, snot-filled world of abject fear and lip-trembling disbelief. Her fears are born not out of the knowledge of a newly-discovered daughter but from having to confront the historic abuse she suffered when she was fifteen. It's just one of a raft of brilliant performances that grace this slice of late twentieth century kitchen sink drama. Timothy Spall, as Cynthia's calm and collected younger brother Maurice, holds the piece together as the likeable arbiter who balances the uncrossed line between his sister and his childless wife Monica (Phyllis Logan). Marianne Jean-Baptiste, as Cynthia's newly-found daughter, is serious and sincere and, once placed within the centre of her birth mother's ill-timed deception, she is completely out of her depth in the most awkward of awkward family get-togethers.

Beautiful, honest and intricately constructed, like its innovative director, the film remains an important piece of British cinematic history.

14: Shane's World

One beat, two beat, three beat, sugar beat. Four beat, five beat,
six beat, wheat-a-beat. Seven beat, eight beat, nine beat,
heartbeat. My heartbeat, my heart is beating for you.
A Room for Romeo Brass (1999)

In 1999's *A Room for Romeo Brass*, the titular character (Andrew Shim) bemoans to his best friend Knocks (Ben Marshall) that he's once again eaten much more than his fair share of the family chip shop order on the way back home to his expectant mum and sister.

> Romeo: Look at them, [referring to the diminished bags
> of chips], look at how small they are. I'm gonna get
> battered. I do this, aww, why have I done it again?

(pause)

Knocks: Because you're fat.

Though that particular film takes us to some dark places later on, that snapshot is largely representative of the kind of work we have come to expect from its highly responsive director, Shane Meadows. It's at once mundane, while also being slightly ridiculous. It's funny and grubby and charming and instantly watchable. Vicky McClure says:

> Shane is completely unique in the way he works, he
> creates an environment that I believe is perfect for actors
> to explore their characters without the strain of hitting
> marks on the floor, remembering lines and being pushed
> for time, provides a freedom you don't always get. Shane
> has always followed his gut instinct so every day is
> different and you very rarely know what's coming next,
> which usually produces a true reaction in front of camera.

According to his website biography, Uttoxeter-born teenager Shane Meadows failed his O-levels and entered into a short-lived and somewhat comical life of crime, which apparently incorporated custard tart theft and the handling of a stolen John Lowe dart set. The young reprobate's criminal adventures petered out when his misdemeanours were met with public derision at an embarrassing court case hearing. The ineptitude of his criminality was possibly the inspiration for his early film *Small Time* (1996).

Volunteering his services for free at Nottingham company Intermedia Film and Video Ltd in exchange for use of their equipment, Meadows was able to experiment with filmmaking, quickly learning the technicalities and at the same time developing his own style. His early films were short, often quirky piss-takes of fly-on-the-wall documentaries or television commercials, usually involving friends and family in lieu of professional actors. His early experiments led to the twelve-minute black and white *Where's the Money, Ronnie?* (1996), a nifty narrative about four petty criminals being interviewed by the police after a murder. A sort of *Reservoir Dogs* meets *Bronco Bullfrog*, its back-to-basics style is stripped and unimpeded by the unnecessary pretension often employed in more stateside indie fare. It is refreshing and ballsy, somehow managing to be unashamed without being the least bit smug. Even its Kurosawa influences are kept in check, its minimal yet pacy editing and handheld camera work ensure that its quirkiness and well-chosen musical interludes perfectly complement the rapidly-evolving Meadows style of storytelling.

Drawing the attention of the wider media for the first time, *Where's the Money, Ronnie?* led to Meadows being commissioned by Channel 4, for whom he made the bare-knuckle boxing documentary *King of the Gypsies*. The pay-out from this work enabled him to fund *Small Time*. With a runtime of just under an hour, this was his first venture into a more feature-like production. The film, written during his lunch breaks, was similar to *Where's the Money, Ronnie?* in that it centred around the lives of a tight-knit band of small-time crooks in a working-class locale, this time shot in and around Sneinton, Nottingham. Like his previous film it melded harshness and comedy together, in an often slightly awkward yet entertaining manner. Meadows himself provided many of the more laugh-out-loud on screen moments when portraying Jumbo, decked out as he is in a ridiculous wavy blonde granny wig.

Though *Small Time* is an amusing well-made micro-budget feature, an effective East Midlands-based companion piece to Forsyth's much earlier *That Sinking Feeling*, it was Meadows' next film, his first proper feature-length production, that began to open the doors to wider public recognition.

By the mid-90s, Bob Hoskins, perhaps unfairly, was largely perceived as that annoying 'It's good to talk' bloke from the BT commercials and a slightly laughable figure in the *Super Mario Bros.* movie. And yet *The Long Good Friday* star had always seemed to eschew any form of typecasting, turning his well-honed acting chops to the multi-award-winning, critically-acclaimed material like *Mona Lisa* (1986), Spielberg's *Hook* (1991), Oliver Stone's *Nixon* (1995), and of course *Who Framed Roger Rabbit?* (1988). But for many, it was his beautifully natural performance as Darcy that helped re-establish his credibility in the minds of British critics and fans alike.

Darcy is the tragic central figure in *Twenty-Four Seven* (1997). The film depicts a community decimated by political hardship and the divisions which bubble to the surface as a result of that deprivation. It focuses on two rival gangs of young adults. Though not particularly bad in nature, boredom and their own sense of nothingness, staring into a futureless void of manky fish fingers and Giro cheques, leads them to a barely stitched-together existence of petty crime and casual violence. When we first meet Darcy, he has been reduced to a physical wreck, a tramp-like drunk, barely able to speak, reduced to living in an abandoned railway carriage, a stinking mound of misplaced hope. The story, shot in stark black and white, takes us back in time before Darcy's downfall and we are presented with a series of flashbacks using diary entry voiceovers in a carefully-constructed narrative which builds into a disastrous and heartbreaking climax.

Darcy, an ex-boxer turned trainer and undying optimist, can see the damage that years of hardship have done to the community which surrounds him. In an effort to turn the mindset of two young gangs into something more positive, he decides to set up a boxing club, figuring that if he can focus their attentions on something healthier they will learn to respect not only other people but themselves. After some initial reluctance both gangs agree to Darcy's proposal and the young men become allies brought together by an upcoming boxing competition and Darcy's motivational fervour and father-like appeal.

In one scene, which is touching yet deliberately unsentimental, Darcy comes to the aid of drug-addled gang member, Fagash. Bathing him and seeing him to bed, he stays with him all night. The seemingly-broken young man, reduced to a life of grotty bedsit squalor and the numbing appeal of narcotic concoctions, is on the verge of nihilistic demise until Darcy steps into to offer support and patriarchal assistance.

In a turn of events which occured in many of the director's later productions, the unity of the gang and the balance that Darcy has introduced into their lives is offset as the boxing competition approaches. Darcy's actions are marred by hard man criminal Ronnie, who opportunistically sees the event as a means to push his awkward son Tonka forward as well as making a few quid on the side. But a more insidious form of disruption comes in the form of Geoff (Bruce Jones). Geoff regularly beats his wife Pat and is openly abusive to son Tim. His cowardice and bitterness froth over in a fit of resentment when he begins to see that Tim may have found something in 'Darcy's group of monkeys' which has always eluded him: a reason for living. His jealousy, vile spitting cynicism and nicotine-yellow finger pointing erupts into a bloody confrontation on the night of the boxing bout.

The two gangs have now come together as a rallying team but they are no match for the rival visiting boxing contenders. Seeing their frustrations explode into ringside scraps, Geoff uses the destructive atmosphere to goad an off-guard and unsettled Darcy into a battle which results in the two of them coming together in a raging tussle. In a shocking scene, which sees Darcy's sensibility, warmth and clear-headedness wiped off the face of the earth by Geoff's own undying brand of Special Brew-tainted verbal hatred, we are treated to an unflinching few minutes of brutality. The brutality is not just in the show of physical aggression which uncomfortably depicts Geoff being pulverised by Darcy in a nearby skip, but in the realisation that Darcy, the carer, the social worker, the trainer, the father, the inspiration is, in the end, no less susceptible to the cruelty which surrounds him than anyone else. He has, as a barely conscious Geoff points out, face mashed beyond recognition, 'fucking lost it.' The tragedy redoubles itself just moments later when Tim, barely able to take in Darcy's Hyde-like transformation, rushes to the aid of his battered biological father, realising that the other man he's perhaps come to see as something better, more humane, is maybe something worse.

It's a moment of cruelty, harsh and unquestionably difficult and it's the kind of gut-wrenching scene we have come to expect from Meadows' films. And yet, unlike other directors who may like to leave us with that cruelty, there is always a warmth which accompanies the bleakness of his stories. The warmth in *Twenty-Four Seven* comes not only in the form of naturalistic dialogue and earthy banter but also in the neatly played out denouement where we see a community coming together at Darcy's funeral. It gives them and us the chance to celebrate not the more animalistic qualities of human behaviour we may have been witness to, but the promise of goodness which also exists within each and every one of us, the importance of having Darcy's often-talked-about 'something to believe in', if only for a short time.

Twenty-Four Seven was not the last time that Meadows played with the idea of absent or uncaring fathers being replaced by flawed surrogates. Indeed, it was a motif which underscored much of his work, from *Dead Man's Shoes* (2004) to *This is England* (2006), but that is not to say that his films are in any sense predictable. In fact, it is the unpredictability, usually in the form of unusual situations, odd pairings or the juxtaposition of humour, vernacular and tragedy which make his work worthy of critical acclaim.

Bob Hoskins returned to Shane Meadows' next film in a much smaller role, almost a cameo. Instead, much of the remaining young cast was selected from Nottingham's Television Workshop. Amongst them were a fifteen-year-old Vicky McClure and Andrew Shim (both featured together again in the later film *This is England*) but Paddy Considine's turn as the warped Morell, in an outstanding debut performance, dominated much of *A Room for Romeo Brass*.

When Gavin (AKA Knocks) is confronted by two youths who mock him because of his back injuries, he is defended once again by best mate Romeo, but when things turn more violent, they are aided by the passing Morell, who sees off their would-be aggressors. Morell cuts an immediately odd figure, gangly, gormless, grown-up and child, impossibly world-weary and stupidly naïve. His manner and weird means of communication, replete with an oddly out-of-place accent which manages to be both confident and insecure at the same time, place him out of the reach of most human beings. From the outset, we understand that he will always be viewed as a freak or, as Vicky McClure's character Ladine neatly sums up, a complete gizzoid.

His laughable belief in his martial arts capabilities and his attempts to chat up Ladine cement him as a gullible idiot clown. And it is Considine's considerable talents which help to build this illusion, till he pulls out the reveal which leaves us staggering and uncertain as to where the film will take us for the rest of its ninety-minute run time. This reveal comes when the two boys accompany Morell on a day trip to the seaside. Though slightly unsure of their older companion at first, Romeo has grown to like him and respect him to a certain degree — a seemingly good-natured if slightly confusing replacement father figure. Knocks though, who is already a much more acerbic character than his friend, has much less time for this strange interloper. Morell, sensing this, sets about placing a barrier between the two friends. Still mulling over an earlier joke which Knocks has played on him, humiliating him in front of his would-be girlfriend Ladine, Morell confronts him about it while Romeo is away buying ice cream. Though it begins as an honest conversation, with Morell offering to give Knocks the chance to clear the air between them, it soon turns nasty when Morell flips from affable buffoon to violent adult abuser, pulling a knife on the terrified child. It's an incredible scene, its power still rings true even after repeated viewings and it's a testament to Considine and Meadows, not only because it's perfectly captured but because we never see it coming.

Unaware of this confrontation, Romeo is frustrated by Knocks's cold attitude towards Morell and soon the division between the friends grows wider, until their contact is reduced to zero when Knocks is admitted to hospital for a long-awaited operation. In the absence of Knocks, Morell gains a tighter control over Romeo, grooming him to the point where his young victim even begins to question his own family — already fractured by the unwelcome return of his estranged father.

Interestingly, Meadows and co-scriptwriter Paul Fraser explore the impact of absent fathers in one sense or another on many levels in *A Room for Romeo Brass*. Morell's own father is dead, and yet he is haunted by the thought of him, the house where he lives is little more than an untouched museum, the dusty rooms bear no signs of Morell's own personality or influence and we begin to wonder what sort of relationship — if any — existed between them. And though Romeo's father has been physically absent for much of his life and there is little willingness on Romeo's part to establish any father/child bond, it is arguable that his presence and influence have a greater impact than that of Knocks's father who may be physically present yet remains emotionally absent. In one scene Knocks's father leaves his son's sickbed to watch an inane sitcom.

Having wormed his way into Romeo's life, seemingly using him as a way to strike up a sexual relationship with sister Ladine, Morell asks her out on a date. She accepts, we suspect, more out of sympathy than genuine attraction. The date is a predictably awkward affair, a scene which has us both wanting to laugh and also call social services. Morell is creepily out of his depth, seemingly unaware of etiquette or what a date is. In a pre-seduction pep talk with himself, virgin Morell exclaims, 'She's a baby chicken and you're a fox, circling her, waiting to go in for the kill...'. It's more #*metoo* than Mills and Boon. And when he strips to his underwear and urges Ladine to 'touch it' we know this will not end well. Fortunately, Ladine is never less than in charge and she escapes the scene at least physically unscathed.

Rejected, Morell takes out his rage out on the one thing weaker than himself: Romeo, a vulnerable child. Soon after though, his already odd behaviour appears to spiral into a kind of psychosis and he attacks a customer who has taken a shine to Ladine, almost beating him to death in front of the terrified Romeo. But when he threatens Knocks's father Bill, he is taken out by Joe, Romeo's father.

As with *Twenty-Four Seven* the discomfort is tempered by the use of humour and recognisable and relatable depictions of working-class family life. Not only that, the childhood bond which exists between the two central characters will feel instantly familiar to many of us who remember those endless summer holidays, where we seemed to laugh longer and harder than we ever did when we were at school. Despite the darkness and the uneasiness of Morell's troubled mind, brilliantly portrayed by Considine, it is permeated by warmth and nostalgia, but it is a less romanticised version not afraid to take the piss out of itself, and its depictions are wholly unpatronising. It's a beautifully-made film which shows us what can happen when something ugly threatens, but it also allows to see beyond that ugliness into another Friday night chip shop run with your best mate in tow, because it'll soon be Saturday again.

There were no such fuzzy feelings to be had in 2004's *Dead Man's Shoes*. Richard, a ruthlessly pragmatic ex-soldier, returns to his home town to look after mentally disabled brother Anthony. But as with other Meadows vehicles, the main characters are haunted by ghosts of the past. Richard is tortured by flashbacks of tragic events and upon his arrival he unleashes a devastating campaign of murderous revenge on a two-bit gang of petty thieves and drug dealers.

> God will forgive and he will allow them into heaven. I
> can't live with that.

Co-written by Meadows and Considine, who also stars as Richard in a career-defining performance, it melds together influences like *Get Carter* and Fincher's *Seven* and plonks the action firmly at the heart of a run-down East Midlands working-class town. It's an entertaining, if sickeningly realised serial killer picture which raises questions about morality and right and wrong, and explores issues like mental health and PTSD and the worryingly easy nature of mob rule and its catastrophic consequences.

More fun was to be had though with *Northern Soul*, a short film Meadows made with Toby Kebbell, Considine's co-star in *Dead Man's*

Shoes. It hilariously depicts the squeaky-voiced protagonist Mark Sherbert's quest to become an all-in wrestler — a task for which he is neither mentally nor physically prepared. In the typically offbeat fashion of the director's early work the piece even includes a bonkers *Rocky*-style training montage, incorporating the eponymous hero's ill-thought-out fitness regime. Predictably, his dreams, not to mention his body, are given a serious beating when he is defeated easily in his first fight. But brilliantly as ever, even amidst the ridiculousness of the situation, Meadows manages to bring out the simple humanity in his leading man. He may be preposterous, sitting alone in the closing moments of the film, decked out in caveman outfit, sipping pathetically at a sherry glass, but we still feel for him. As in *Dead Man's Shoes*, music provides an important anchor. Meadows even brings three-piece outfit Clayhill into the narrative when they make an appearance as the pub band, providing a live soundtrack to the action. It's a moment which almost breaks the fourth wall but not quite, and it's a construct which the director brought to bear at the close of his next film, which, like its 70s counterpart *Quadrophenia*, came crashing into the cinemas as a *bona fide* British cult classic.

This is England (2006) never allows us not to be involved. From its Toots and the Maytals-scored opening montage incorporating grainy period TV footage, segueing the likes of Roland Rat, Ronald Reagan, Thatcher and *Knight Rider* into some sort of rocksteady beat-fuelled 80s fever dream, to its heart-busting, violent climax and straight-to-camera accusatory denouement, it simply never lets us go. Its largely young cast decked out in skinhead finery, a blaze of Ben Sherman, Doc Martens and fishnets present a refreshing alternative to more inelegant or romanticised views of British estate kids. Working-class and balancing at the edge of a UK counterculture, they are neither villainous nor heroic, but rather bonded together by circumstance, schooling, environment and a new decade of greed and control, their red braces worn in *A Clockwork Orange* mock defiance of stock market traders and yuppie vacuity.

The film, apparently partly autobiographical, centres around the picked-on and fatherless schoolkid Shaun (Thomas Turgoose). The scrawny thirteen-year-old finds day-to-day life difficult, with no money for the latest more fashionable non-flared trousers — 'Woodstock's that way pal' — and with his widowed mum working long hours, he often finds himself drifting friendless between the classroom and yet another violent encounter with sarcastic playground loudmouth Harvey. His life, though, takes on a new shape when he is taken under the wing of Woody (Joe Gilgun) and his gang. His new set of mates, a rowdy but good-as-gold mob of skinheads and alternative types, induct Shaun into their simple yet fun way of living. As a unit they shrug off boredom and lack of cash by sticking together and amusing themselves the best way they can, throwing makeshift parties or smashing the hell out of abandoned buildings. Shaun is not only given a boost in terms of his outlook on life, he is also given a physical makeover by the gang, who shave his unkempt locks to give him a grade 1 suedehead trim, his flares and anorak replaced by Levi jeans, Ben Sherman shirt and jet black Crombie. It is only after his transformation is complete — 'Honestly, you look absolutely sterling, mate' — that he is introduced to Combo (Stephen Graham).

Combo, recently released from prison, is an older member of the gang. While Woody and co. have come to the skinhead scene off the back of more recent modern trends via the Ska and Mod revival waves, Combo is an original. And while Woody's gang is inherently good-natured, their attraction to the scene is about music and image and having a laugh. Combo though, while incarcerated, has developed more unhealthy attitudes to race and culture.

'Are you a proper little skinhead then, eh?' he asks on their first meeting, Shaun's more grown-up look marred by the fact that he has chocolate-smeared lips, reminding us that this is still a highly impressionable child. Combo's reappearance and his questionable attitudes to race soon cause uneasiness, particularly with Milky (Andrew Shim), the only black member of the gang. The divisions turn into a catastrophic split when Combo calls them to a special meeting at his run-down house, where he wheels out his raging manifesto.

> Two thousand years this little tiny fucking island has been raped and pillaged, by people who have come here and wanted a piece of it — two fucking world wars! Men have laid down their lives for this. For this... and for what? So people can stick their fucking flag in the ground and say, 'Yeah! This is England. And this is England, and this is England.'

The lines are drawn then, quite literally in gob, across Combo's filthy living room floor. Each member of the gang is forced to pick a side —

Woody's more benevolent group or Combo's distinct brand of unfocused racism. Much to the astonishment of Woody and Lol (Vicky McClure), Shaun decides to remain with Combo.

It is here that the film takes us on a darker journey as 'nice lad' Shaun, under the tutelage of unsound patriarch Combo, is dragged into a vile world of prejudice and racist attacks. Not only does Shaun attend a National Front meeting, he also helps Combo and co. to rob the local corner shop, verbally assaulting its Asian owner.

And yet, because of Stephen Graham's extraordinary performance under the careful direction of Meadows, Combo never comes across as simplistic. His political standpoint may sit a million miles from our own and his actions may be repellent, but we are never presented with an unthinking stereotype. His angry and confused state, in part elevated by his sense of abandonment, not only by an absent father but by a system represented by 'that Thatcher who sits in her fucking ivory tower', is explored much more eloquently here than perhaps it would have been under a less nuanced filmmaker. While Meadows never attempts to align our sympathies with Combo's fractured form of racism, we are encouraged to see him as a human being, and the relationship which forms between himself and Shaun is believable if deeply troubling.

Having been spurned by Lol, who is now in a relationship with Woody, Combo hooks up with the estranged Milky and for a while they share a bag of weed and listen to the music which had bonded them in the first place, and it looks as though a new harmony has developed between the two men. However, Combo becomes ill at ease when Milky begins to relate stories about his own family. Incensed by his own lack of family support, frustration explodes into a sickeningly violent scene where he half beats Milky to death in front of a terrified Shaun.

The film is brought to a beautifully realised close with Shaun throwing a crumpled St George flag into the open sea in front of him before turning directly to the audience and defiantly staring us down. It's a powerful ending, and it has become decidedly more uncomfortable in recent times when race and immigration scares are ramped up into paranoid media campaigns which seek to exploit the displaced and weary in dangerous political gameplay.

Shane Meadows remains an important British film-maker. His output, including the films discussed here and the *This is England* TV show, which will be talked about more in chapter sixteen, provides a unique brand of social realism, which may be influenced by, say, Ken Loach, but is never anything less than the director's own. Those like me, who were brought up in council housing or come from working-class backgrounds, will immediately recognise something in his films, see their complexity, their simplicity, their truth. It's life that comes served in crumpled newspaper, sprinkled with batter bits, flavoured with salt, vinegar and gravy, it's knowing you've not got enough, and squaring it anyway, it's trying to make the best of it and having a mate who will always take the piss but sometimes bring it back.

15: From Babylon to Beautiful Laundrettes

I believe one should fight for what one believes. Provided one is
absolutely sure one is absolutely right.

To Sir, with Love (1967)

When the troopship Empire Windrush docked in Kingston, Jamaica in
1948, to pick up servicemen on leave, it was bound for England. Initially
it was far from full but as word about the trip spread, largely via an
opportunistic spot of advertising selling tickets for the voyage from £28,
its hull was soon at capacity. Various reports claim that its estimated
passenger list came in somewhere around the eight hundred mark.

When the ship's passengers, largely West Indians, many of whom had
fought in World War II, disembarked at Tilbury, it was immediately a
newsworthy and controversial event. It was the first wave of black
immigrants, and their influence on art, music, culture and food would
play an important part in the transformation of the UK from its tired
grey post-war state into a more vibrant, colourful future.

In the mid-50s, Tory Minister Enoch Powell openly invited workers
from the Caribbean, mainly young women, to train as nurses for the
fledgling NHS hospitals, now desperate for trained professionals to cope
with the demand of patients, who for the first time were now in receipt
of health care free at the point of service. Though the take-up calls for
labour were minimal, by 1958 only around 125,000 had answered the
call. Other factors, though, would encourage more Caribbean
immigrants to take up residence in the UK.

In truth, for many Caribbean islanders who were seeking to settle in
another country, the US had always been a preferred destination, but in
1952 the McCarran-Walter act, which reinforced the controversial
system of immigrant selection, severely restricted the number of
Caribbeans entering the US.

With the American door shut many turned to the UK, largely because
before the Commonwealth Immigrants Act of 1962 was passed, all
Commonwealth citizens were given the status of British citizenship.
Inevitably though, a sourness crept into the narrative and an insidious
wave of negativity was aimed at the new arrivals, despite the fact that they
were part of a much-needed new workforce. Enoch Powell, whose
previous open arms had turned to shaking fists with his 'As I look ahead
I am filled with foreboding' — Rivers of Blood speech, would help fuel a
growing wave of racism across the country.

Despite popular belief, immigrants who had been in the country less than five years were denied access to council housing, and as there were then no anti-discrimination laws, private landlords were allowed to openly refuse immigrant tenants from taking up their accommodation, 'No coloureds' and 'No West Indians' signs affixed to properties were a common sight. As a result, many immigrants were forced into run-down areas, finding themselves at the mercy of slum landlords. Despite the damaging and unforgivable aspects of discrimination and institutionally ingrained racism, black people sought solace and protection within their own communities and a stronger identity was forged with immigrants developing a unity regardless of their original class or background.

This side of British history in the making was barely touched upon in mainstream cinema or television. Although there were (now largely forgotten) films which at least tried to highlight the issues and throw light upon the lot of black immigrants or visitors, including Basil Dearden's *Pool of London* (1951) and Roy Ward Baker's ITV production *Flame in the Streets* (1961), there was little in the way of true black representation which reflected the changing nature of the country and its make-up of citizens. It was as though the film industry was in denial of what was happening just beyond its celluloid perimeters.

This is not to say that talented black actors were not being utilised at all. Paul Robeson had starred in several British films back in the 1930s and Brock Peters, who had previously played Tom Robinson in Robert Mulligan's *To Kill a Mockingbird* (1962), brought the character of Johnny to life brilliantly in 1962's *The L-Shaped Room*. But it was almost that the American-ness of those two actors and their perceived connection to all things Hollywood cancelled out their 'blackness', at least the kind of blackness that many white British people were beginning to link to a corruption of their national character.

The tentative acceptance of black screen actors grew throughout the 50s and 60s, particularly in the US. Film appearances of established live performers such as Nat King Cole and Sammy Davis Jr helped to paint a more acceptable picture, yet in reality segregation and anti-black feeling was still ingrained within American society. Films like *To Kill a Mockingbird* sought to address this, its 1930s setting being a thinly veiled representation of modern America, yet mostly Hollywood tried to hang on to its whiter-than-white appearance in more ways than one.

In 1965, the 'Long Hot Summer' referred to the 159 race riots which occurred across the US. June and July saw unrest spilling out over cities and states like Tampa, Buffalo, Birmingham, Chicago, New York, Milwaukee, Minneapolis, New Jersey and Detroit. Many young black citizens felt backed into a corner, trapped by threats of violence, actual lynch mobs, out-and-out prejudice and unfathomable levels of inequality. The land of the free was far from that. Uncle Sam may not have asked for a fight but he was getting one.

Films such as *The Defiant Ones* (1958) and *The Intruder* (1962) reflected these societal imbalances and the growing need for revolt which was bubbling beneath the surface, but it took a later Sidney Poitier vehicle, *In the Heat of the Night* (1967), to really start to explore the anger and indignities faced by those who much of America saw as being second-class citizens.

Sidney Poitier also made appearances in UK productions, most notably in the explosive and controversial rock'n'roll scored teen flick *Blackboard Jungle* (1955). Conversely, it was an altogether gentler film which began to plant the seed that fairer black representation on British screens might not be too bad an idea.

To Sir, with Love (1967) has many faults. Though popular with audiences at the time it feels dated now. Its views on women and feminist issues are archaic, replete with talk of sluts and 'sluttish' behaviour and obsession with marriage and babies. It's also a fairly stereotyped and wholly unrealistic portrayal of an inner-city school life, not only are some of the pupils clearly pushing thirty as in *Please Sir*, but the language and the flimsy threats of violence have all the social realism and authenticity of the *Carry On* cast pretending to be hippies at the end of *Carry On Camping*. And yet, this remains an important film, not because of its content or ability to reflect the issues effectively, but because it was there at all. In 2019 we thankfully have much fairer representation of black faces on screen, though there is still much work to be done. But fifty years ago, the fact that a black face was there at all, particularly in a lead role in a British production, was noteworthy in itself. And while the film is no *In the Heat of the Night* — director James Clavell deliberately sought to make something gentler, doggedly ignoring studio requests for rape or violence within the text — it is a very human film.

Poitier is an appealing screen presence. His earlier appearance in *Blackboard Jungle* and his controlled, yet seething portrayal of Mr Tibbs in *In the Heat of the Night* single him out as one of the world's finest actors. And his personal story is far more interesting than anything discussed within the script of *To Sir, with Love*. After being raised in the Bahamas in a family of seven children, Poitier moved to the US in his teens where, to survive the bitter winter, he lied about his age and joined the army. Not feeling suited to the military lifestyle, rather than tell the truth about his age, he decided to act 'insane' instead. He only came clean when the threat of shock therapy was touted. He was released from service a few weeks later. These types of experiences and his poor upbringing certainly help to give his early film appearances authenticity. Though much of *To Sir, with Love* is cringe-worthy, not least the bug-eyed overly-acted innocence of Lulu and her gormless classmates, the same cannot be said for Poitier. While on screen he is never less than completely convincing and, though he may be battling with a fairly tired script and fellow performers, he is undoubtedly a quietly charismatic and memorable character.

Despite the film's popularity driven entirely by the black leading man — a concept which would have been unheard of just a few years before — other films which more realistically reflected 'real life' experiences of black British working class citizens did not surface for a few more years.

Pressure (1976) attempted to explore issues relevant to the 'black experience' including lack of educational opportunity and the cycle of deprivation it led to. The film was unremittingly critical of the system, with particular ire aimed at the police and judicial system. As interesting as the film is, it hardly set the box office on fire, remaining more of a cult, underground feature. It did however star Norman Beaton, who just a year later went on to play the patriarch of a new British sit-com family. *The Fosters* was an ITV show which was based on the American vehicle *Good Times*. It featured a young Lenny Henry in his first regular TV series. It was the precursor to later predominantly black cast shows such as Channel 4's *No Problem* and the highly successful *Desmond's*, also starring Beaton. *The Fosters*, however, only survived for two series. Though it was an admirable attempt to try and integrate black faces into the sea of white-only light entertainment that dominated the schedules, it was lost in an era where offensive output like the highly suspect *Love Thy Neighbour*, *Mind Your Language* and *The Black and White Minstrel Show* still rode untouched on a wave of popularity.

Despite the introduction of the 1976 Race Relations Act, designed to protect people from discrimination on the grounds of race, and counter-cultural movements such as the Two-Tone scene which brought together black and white musicians and mixed-race audiences to dance floors and live venues, the levels of anti-black and Asian feeling and racial clashes were on the rise. The National Front, particularly under the leadership of John Tyndall, sought to exploit immigration fears and marginalise minorities with its thuggish heavy-hammer politics incorporating white supremism, fascism, anti-Semitism and British Nationalism.

Prejudice was not only in the hands of a minority of extremists. The so called 'sus laws' were just one example that illustrated that racism on an official institutional level was alive and well. The 'sus law' of England and Wales was the slang term for 'stop and search' powers originally intended to enable police officers to arrest citizens who were suspected of being in breach of section 4 of the Vagrancy Act of 1894. In practice though, particularly during the 70s and 80s, these powers were often used to target members of the black community or people from ethnic backgrounds. Heavy-handed policing and prejudicial enforcements of the law were parodied perfectly in an early *Not the Nine O'clock News* sketch featuring Rowan Atkinson giving his overly-eager racist charge a dressing down.

> Sergeant: Savage, why do you keep arresting this man?
>
> Constable Savage: He's a villain, sir.
>
> Sergeant: A villain.
>
> Constable Savage: And a jailbird, sir.
>
> Sergeant: I know he's a jailbird, Savage, he's down in the cells now! We're holding him on a charge of being caught in possession of curly black hair and thick lips!

Social deprivation, poor housing, lack of opportunity and racially-motivated attacks which were often ignored or insufficiently followed up by police and authorities became the spark which ignited social unrest in areas like Toxteth and Brixton. The build-up to the heavily-documented rioting encompassing all of the above, plus the clashes between poor blacks and poor whites and inter-generational feuding, were captured brilliantly in Franco Rosso's *Babylon* (1980).

The use of the word Babylon, in Rastafarian terms, describes either a corrupt government system or the guardians of that system, i.e. the police force. Rosso's film of the same name, scripted by Martin Stellman (*Quadrophenia*), explores that definition and examines just how corrupt a place Britain had become, particularly for a young black population, by the end of the 1970s. For many, the dawn of Thatcherism cast a long shadow over an already-faltering country. Unemployment was high, socialist values had taken a severe beating in the 1979 election, which ushered in a newer, crueller form of politics and a Party which was ready to go to war with public services and a then heavily-unionised workforce.

Centring around the character of David, or 'Blue', played by Brinsley Forde, who had risen to fame in *Here Come the Double Deckers* in the early seventies and went on to front reggae band Aswad, *Babylon* not only focused on those government-level inequalities, including police brutality, work-based racism and lack of opportunity, it also examined the societal pressures that manifested under a deeply crooked system that profited highly when ordinary citizens turned on one another. In the film, we see poor people turn against each other, racially-inspired violence, minorities betraying other minorities and friendships torn apart. Interestingly, the film also examines not just white characters turning against black characters but also the mistrust that was developing between first and second generation immigrants. This is highlighted by the relationship between Blue and his father. The older of the two seems incredulous that his son cannot just settle down into a regular job and make the most of what he has been dealt, seemingly oblivious to the levels of prejudice which sit on his doorstep. If his father reflects the need for many first-wave Windrush settlers to assimilate into British culture, Blue represents the desire for many black teenagers and young adults to seek out their ethnic roots and embrace a culture which had been largely left behind by their parents and grandparents.

Where *Quadrophenia* focused on the burgeoning mid-sixties Mod craze, *Babylon* embraced the sound system scene and, more importantly, it centred around the characters who were part of that subculture. We are not presented with the black representations which still dominated a white middle-class media. The teenage protagonists have a genuine love of a music which not only reminds them of where they are from but also what they could be. They have aspirations and hopes in the same way that anyone has and yet their particular dreams are made even more unattainable by an increasingly racist environment. Though the garage lockup where they store their sound system equipment is dark, damp and dingy, it also represents the one space in which they can be completely free. This is made all the more tragic when it is broken into and vandalised by a local gang of National Front thugs.

In the final moments of the film, the authorities descend on a party to make a series of arrests, but in a last act of defiance which is both depressing and empowering, the rock steady beats grow louder and louder drowning out the sirens of the police cars outside. The fight will go on.

The break-up the British Empire and the independence of countries which made up the South Asian subcontinent saw a post-war rise in the levels of immigrants from India, Pakistan, Sri Lanka and later Bangladesh settling in the UK. Another wave of immigrants came in 1972 when South Asians were expelled from Uganda by despot Idi Amin. Like the West Indians who had made the UK their home, they became a vital part of the workforce and, like their West Indian counterparts, they were able to bring fresh new aspects to the British landscape which helped shape a multicultural future. The positive effect that South Asians had on the British economy was unquestionable. Many from that community helped to revolutionise a staid retail industry and their expertise within the NHS was of paramount importance.

Predictably, though, at the time, many Asians were faced with considerable home-grown opposition and a kind of frothing racism which had been inspired by the National Front and Tory war-horse Enoch Powell.

While *Babylon* chronicled the UK's skidding car crash into Thatcherism, documenting its concussed state of confusion and its foggy-headed attitude towards immigration and working-class values, the ensuing years saw the rise of neo-liberalism, privatisation and thinly-veiled racism and homophobia ushered in as political policy. By 1985, Thatcher was well into her second term as Prime Minister. The industrial landscape of Britain had been devastated by cuts, working-class communities mainly in the North and the Midlands had been brought to their knees and the miners had suffered a monumental defeat. For many, the writing was on the wall.

And while swathes of the mainstream press seemed happy with this state of affairs, elsewhere, particularly in the world of film, TV and comedy, the knives were out. Channel 4 had shaken up the world of UK broadcasting with its own brand of radical programming, the BBC had commissioned hard-hitting dramas like Alan Bleasdale's *Boys from the Black Stuff* and a fresh form of stand-up, dubbed 'alternative comedy', was blazing a politically-charged trail across the country.

On the other side of the coin, many parts of Britain were being swayed by the promise of private wealth and the 'look after yourself' form of rhetoric. Social housing was placed on the market as part of the controversial 'right to buy' scheme. Once-nationalised utilities like British Gas were about to be sold off and the Yuppies with their Gordon Gekko-inspired 'greed is good' mantra were now a recognisable group, images of their designer suits and brick-like mobile phones were used as ballast between the news stories of IRA terrorism and threats of World War Three.

My Beautiful Laundrette (1985), 'a grim fairy-tale' directed by Stephen Frears and written by Hanif Kureishi, managed to capture this odd and unsettling time in British history.

Young Pakistani Omar (Gordon Warnecke), looks after his father, 'Papa' (Roshan Seth), an aging alcoholic left-leaning thinker, whose grey-eyed, ghost-like countenance seems to reflect the fading spectre of socialist values which haunts the modern free-market system. Despite Papa's wish to see his son aspire to more intellectual pursuits — 'We must have knowledge, we all must if we are to understand what is being done and to whom' — Omar is tempted by the lure of quick money and fast cars and is soon drawn into Uncle Nasser's (Saeed Jaffrey) much more cynical entrepreneurial web — 'In this damn country which we hate and love, you can get anything you want, it's all spread out and available. That's why I believe in England. Only you have to know how to squeeze the tits of the system.'

Omar is also gay; he begins a relationship with old school friend and one-time National Front lout Johnny (Daniel Day-Lewis) and together they set up and run Powders, a neon-lit, swish laundrette, a dazzling shrine set against the backdrop of grey skies and manky-looking South London tower blocks.

At one point Omar is described by a relative as being an 'in-between' — a soul who is finding it difficult to belong to any one group — and this could be extended to many characters within the text. They all seem to struggle to accept an identity, all trying to adapt a way of being which usually clashes with either conscience or background, a motif which perfectly encapsulates the duplicitous nature of the Thatcher/Reagan-dominated era. The laundrette represents an ideal — a space where classes can come together, where gays and straights can mingle and where race is no longer an issue. Unfortunately, it's at a point in time where that ideal can only ever be a brightly-lit short-lived fantasy. The fairy tale is brought to an end as a dustbin smashes through the window of the besieged shop front. Elsewhere we get glimpses of the reality behind the fantasy — the money which funds the business comes largely from illegal drug smuggling and dodgy property dealing, where the unfortunate casualties are immigrants and the poor. Characters in the film take great delight in steamrollering any aspirations which don't involve getting rich at another's expense. Class, art, literature and ethnicity are marginalised throughout the film, just as they were under Tory rule. At one point a Rastafarian poet is mercilessly thrown to the streets, his books cast to the wind. It's a fascinating look at the mid-80s, it's a product of its time and a brilliantly smart reflection. Eerily, in these strange days of heightened tensions, right-wing extremists and Brexit clashes, it's still relevant.

The theme of identity was also key to Damien O'Donnell's *East is East* (1999), though it was made some fourteen years after *My Beautiful Laundrette*. The film is set in Salford, Greater Manchester in 1971, a year before the Ugandan exiles came. It focuses on chip shop owner George Khan (Om Puri), a Pakistani who has been in the UK since 1937. Though he has a wife back in his country of birth, he is now married to Ella (Linda Bassett), a Roman Catholic. Their seven children, though, largely identify with English culture, and with the exception of Maneer, reject their heritage, much to George's belligerent objections. *East is East* works because it is not afraid to handle the complexities and nuances of class, race, culture, religion and generational difference. The film begins with the family (*sans* George) taking part in an Easter Day parade. Their enjoyment of the event comes out of the fact that it's a fun occasion, a street party, devoid of any heavily religious significance. But as George returns from town, the children scatter, fearing they will catch his proud yet foul-mouthed Islamic tirade. In another scene, Tariq (Jimi Mistry), Meenah (Archie Panjabi) and Abdul (Raji James) are seen surreptitiously cooking and eating pork sausages in George's absence — another act of defiance which is less to do with rejecting Muslim values than with objecting to their own father's tyrannical pressure. In a desperate effort to alleviate some of the shame he feels after son Saleem runs away from the family to avoid his wedding, George stubbornly redoubles his efforts to prepare the marriages of his two remaining eldest sons, much to the consternation of Ella, who is losing patience with his heavy-handed approach, and groom-to-be Tariq — 'I'm not marrying a fucking Paki' — objects most vehemently to his father's machinations. Strangely, his need to rebel is pitched at the same level as his father's need to conform to Islamic tradition, they perhaps share much in common on more levels than they would care to admit. Tariq adopts the name Tony, has a white girlfriend and employs an inward form of racism aimed at his own brother Maneer (Emil Marwa), who he dubs Gandhi, in an odd echo of white prejudice which lazily lumps in all South Asians together as an indistinguishable mass. And yet, like Arthur Seaton before him, we get the feeling that Tariq is beyond politics or race relations. His need is not to identify with either British culture or his Pakistani heritage, it is simply to be young, pissed and sexually active.

There are many funny and beautifully-realised moments in the film which pinpoint the pleasures and pains of culture clash. In one such scene tomboy Meenah, who has previously objected to wearing traditional dress, re-enacts a perfectly choreographed Bollywood dance routine. The fact that she's performing the show with a broom in her hands, wearing wellies, whilst her brothers gut cod in the back yard of the chip shop, only serves to highlight the delight to be had from seamlessly bringing together two distinctly separate ways of life, the perceived distance and difference between the foreign or exotic and down-to-earth working-class existence disappears before our eyes. In another scene, Sajid, the youngest of the family, forever hiding beneath the hood of his scruffy parka, is dragged off to hospital for a belated circumcision. On his return home, feeling more than a little sorry for himself, his neighbour 'aunty' Anna wittily refers to his father's gift of a new watch and dressing gown as being 'not much of a swap' and again, an earthy English humour plays hand in hand with a more foreign outlook without skipping a beat.

The film takes on a darker turn, particularly in the moments of domestic violence, when a humiliated George, broken by his own perceived sense of dishonour, attacks Ella behind the counter of the chip shop. Ironically, the only son in the film to suffer the full wrath of George's anger is Abdul, the most devout and loyal member of his offspring. With George, we witness a man in rapid decline, a figure who is out of touch not because of his religion or culture but because of his own sour sense of non-achievement, finding it easier to lash out rather than begin to question his own list of failures. He is also so focused on the supposed 'treachery' at the hands of his sons and daughter that he is unable to grasp the fullness of his own betrayals, especially of Ella and Maneer.

16: A Woman's Work

You gotta laugh ain't ya sweetheart? Else you'd cry.
Secrets and Lies (1996)

'I 'ave 'ad a few reactions,' said Andrea Dunbar in a 1987 edition of BBC1's *Look North*, 'but I don't think it's nothing to worry about. I've only 'ad three people complain. You know, it's not bad off an 'ole estate, is it?' She was speaking about the film adaptation of *Rita, Sue and Bob Too*, which though she co-wrote, she would later disown due the interference of other writers.

Her original play follows the lives of two girls who, like Jo from *A Taste of Honey* before them, are about to leave school to face a not-so-promising future. They find temporary respite in weekend babysitting duties for Bob and Michelle, whose own tastefully-decorated semi on the posh estate, with its fully-stocked fridge and other comforts, provides an altogether more affluent environment than the squalid housing conditions in which the girls currently reside. Things get more complicated when Bob starts a clandestine sexual relationship with both Rita and Sue during a late-night excursion when he is meant to be driving the impressionable pair home.

What transpires is a funny, raw and messily detailed story of estate life which incorporates sex, infatuation, betrayal and teenage pregnancy and yet it never feels forced or 'worthy' in any sense. This is not a tale which desperately needed to be told, nor is it an angry indictment in the Ken Loach sense, it is simply an honest portrayal of an on-the-breadline existence, stripped of any politically correct pandering or the need to be edgy or satirical. It simply is what it is. And whatever that 'it' is, it is brought to us originally via the untampered-with voice of an authentically working-class woman.

I recently spoke to writer, ethnographer and outspoken Class War campaigner, Lisa McKenzie, about what she perceived Dunbar's original play had been about, and what she made of more recent middle-class perceptions of the piece either as film or play:

> I went to see *Rita, Sue and Bob Too* at the Royal Court a couple of weeks ago. That was fucking depressing. It was actually one of the most depressing nights I've had for a long time, it really upset me. It didn't sit right with me. Andrea Dunbar wrote that not as a play about abuse but

actually just a play about the reality of two girls' lives but the audience watched it as abuse and that's what upset me. The audience couldn't understand that [Rita and Sue] were having a laugh…

Andrea Dunbar was raised on the Buttershaw council estate in Bradford, West Yorkshire. Daughter to two textile factory workers, she did not exactly fit the image of the modern playwright. She was young, female and from the wrong part of the world, as far as the establishment was concerned. But her uncluttered ability to fashion engaging stories, ripped from the streets of the area she grew up in, soon gained her the attention of supportive teachers, and then of the wider art world. When she was just eighteen, Dunbar's first play, *The Arbor*, was premiered at the Royal Court Theatre. Her initial success echoed that of Delaney's breakthrough with *A Taste of Honey* in the West End just over twenty years before.

The Arbor, about a young girl who falls pregnant to a Pakistani man in a deeply racist environment, was received so well that she was commissioned to write another play, which eventually became *Rita, Sue and Bob Too*.

When that play was adapted for cinema in 1987 it was directed by Alan Clarke (*Scum*, *The Firm*). And as the tagline 'Thatcher's Britain with its knickers down' suggested, it played up the bawdier nature of the original story. Though always intended to be funny, it was the tagged-on happier ending which led to Dunbar falling out with the project. The film, which was shot on and around the Buttershaw estate, Dunbar's old stomping ground, also drew heavy criticism from the residents there for its 'negative portrayals'. And yet despite its faults and it being, in the words of Lisa McKenzie, 'A bit too *Carry On*,' the film proved to be popular and remains a perennial modern classic.

It's regrettable that the film, certainly in the eyes of the original writer, deviated somewhat from the tone of the play, given that then, as now, there were so few working-class female voices coming through the system. However, the film does have its merits. Clarke's direction is uncomplicated and pervasive, and though it is never forced down our throats, the visual reminders of Thatcher's broken Britain and its shell-shocked working-class communities are always there, littered at the periphery of the action. And if Dunbar was unhappy with the finished product, her influence can arguably be seen most acutely in the performances of the lead actresses Siobhan Finneran (Rita) and Michelle Holmes (Sue). Their on-screen partnership is unhindered by sentimentality or the usual enforced character development which permeates needier productions. The two girls make for a believable teenage double act, their crappy home lives making them loyal to each other yet fiercely territorial when they stumble upon a good thing, no matter how dubious or temporary. Their willingness to throw themselves into bed with Bob, who through modern eyes certainly comes across as an abusive adult, is not born out of a lapse of morality or indeed naivety, it's simply an act which affords them a few laughs, a bit of money and brief escape from a future which has already been set in place. It's a standpoint which few middle-class commentators would care to understand.

Tragically, Dunbar would not get to see how her work would endure in British popular culture, as she collapsed of a brain haemorrhage in her local pub in 1990 and died shortly afterwards. She was just twenty-nine. Towards the end, she had been hampered by criticism of *Rita, Sue and Bob Too*, largely from her own community, had sunk into alcoholism and had been investigated for allegedly claiming benefits without declaring royalties. It certainly seems true that her final years were marred by controversy and complications. Her life was examined, some would say uncharitably, in Clio Barnard's uncompromising film *The Arbor* (2010), a documentary which experimentally mixed recorded family member interviews with filmed footage of actors lip-syncing the audio. Barnard also went on to direct *The Selfish Giant*, whose nods to Dunbar's previous work were clear not just in tone and presentation but in other ways too — she calls one of the child protagonists Arbor and also casts Siobhan Finneran of *Rita, Sue and Bob Too*. Dunbar's legacy though, as with Delaney beforehand, was an important one, not only from a female perspective but a class one too.

After getting what she describes as her 'break' in the Shane Meadows feature *A Room for Romeo Brass*, Vicky McClure may have believed she was destined for stardom, and she was right, but her household name status came after a substantial hiatus working at Direct Valuation, a property valuation company, to support her acting career.

At age eleven McClure was enrolled at the Television Workshop in Nottingham, which she later described as being 'truly responsible for the career I have now...' It was a career which saw her go on to act in Madonna's directorial debut *Filth and Wisdom* and placed her as star of BBC1's ratings winner *Line of Duty*. But it was her turn as the troubled Lol, in the Shane Meadows-helmed TV dramas *This is England '86* and

This is England '88, which really saw her bloom into her emotional and brilliant BAFTA-winning best.

The character of Lol began as one the smaller parts in Meadows' *This is England* feature film released in 2006. Girlfriend to Woody (Joe Gilgun), Lol acts as matriarch/big sister to the small band of ragged-arsed skinheads, but it is her previous brief sexual relationship with the troubled Combo, one that he won't forget and she tries not to remember — that adds most to the dynamic of the tense storyline. It's an intense scene, with Combo confronting Lol, and essentially laying out his feelings before her in an increasingly awkward manner. This awkwardness is ramped up further by Meadows, who cleverly films the scene in the confines of a small car, the claustrophobic shot adds to closeness of the feelings being expressed. Lol is able to dismiss his entreaties, quickly and without garbled sentiment. In some ways her words could seem cruel, but this is where the brilliance of McClure shines through, we know that Lol knows that if she gives the fragile Combo any chink of light in regard to a possible relationship between them that it will not end well, that he will bring her as well as himself down. McClure is able to tap into these fears. Lol's sharp rebuttal and quick exit from the vehicle is an act of self-preservation, not a random show of cruelty. We are already aware of the violence Combo is capable of and the unpredictable nature of his personality, and Lol is taking a huge risk in this scene. Both McClure and Graham capture this perfectly, creating a classic sense of polarity — Combo's weakness matched pound for pound by Lol's strength.

When it came to *This is England '86*, the highly-anticipated TV spinoff, Meadows, while retaining his original cast, decided to shine his light on all the characters at his disposal, television giving him a broader canvas on which to paint his kitchen sink stories. Though we still focus on the life of young Shaun (Thomas Turgoose), we gain more understanding of the original film's list of supporting characters such as Gadget (Andrew Ellis), Smell (Rosamund Hanson) and Cynthia (Jo Hartley). We are also introduced to other characters who we only saw glimpses of in the film, such as the comically buxom Trudy (Hannah Walters) and one-time school bully, now paid-up member of Woody's gang, Harvey (Michael Socha). Meadows and co-writer Jack Thorne invite us into the troubled home life of Lol and younger sister Kelly (Chanel Cresswell). Though Lol and Woody are due to be married in the not-so-romantic local community centre, complete with sausage rolls and a meagre selection of guests, things go awry when Meggy (Perry Benson) suffers a heart attack in a public toilet during the nuptials. Forced to put off the wedding, Lol begins to suspect that somehow Woody is relieved by this turn of events. The situation worsens when Lol discovers that her mother, Chrissy, has rekindled her relationship with Mick (Johnny Harris), Lol's estranged father and erstwhile sexual abuser. Sadly, neither Chrissy nor Kelly are able to accept Lol's accusations. Unable to face a future with Woody in his grotty new flat, Lol turns to Milky (Andrew Shim) and sleeps with him.

We are left in no doubt as to the sadistic capabilities of Mick when we are forced to witness him sexually assaulting Trev, Lol's vulnerable younger friend. Brilliantly realised, Meadows took great care in filming the scene, checking in constantly and supportively with his two actors, in order to create something honest, disturbing and not salacious or suggestive. It's difficult to watch, the grubbiness and throwaway nature of Mick's actions as he carelessly destroys a young woman's life while the football playing out on the telly adds to our revulsion. Mick, excellently portrayed by Johnny Harris at his quietly terrifying best, is unquestionably nasty, his lack of empathy for another person is staggering. And yet he is also a human being and family man, as abusers often are, and it is that duality, which is focused on here so acutely, that cements the realism within the drama. Mick, carefully written by Thorne and Meadows and played by Harris, is an embodiment of the calculating sex offender, his very presence an enigma, at once loving dad and husband but also a behind-closed-doors monster. The show forces us to recognise this unpalatable daily reality. As Anna Graves, specialist trauma and sexual abuse counsellor, told me:

> Placed within a societal context, *This Is England '86* aired in 2010. Just two years later, in 2012, the Savile case hit the headlines; forcing us, as a society, to acknowledge the many ways child sexual abuse occurs in the UK; and leading to the formation of IICSA (Independent Inquiry into Childhood Sexual Abuse). Through creating *This Is England '86*, Meadows helped us face society's last sexual taboo.

But it is the climax of the first series which places Lol back into the centre of the action. Having found out that her father has raped Trev, she confronts him, but when he also tries to sexually assault her she kills him with a hammer. After Combo takes the blame for her and goes to prison, Lol is left in a state of bewilderment and guilt.

The second series, *This is England '88*, catches up with her two years later. Now saddled with Milky's child and stuck in a run-down flat, Lol, haunted by the ghost of Mick and the murder for which she has allowed someone else to shoulder the blame, begins to fall into deep depression and worsening mental health. While other storylines play out, there is no question that our grim fascination is definitely with McClure. It is an incredible performance.

McClure viscerally captures the dismantling of a human being via a traumatic series of events. Her unravelling sanity is shown with all its numbness, darkness, post-natal depression, and terrifyingly bleak, half-dreamed visions of the past intact. Spurred on by guilt and insomnia, her breakdown spills into snot-filled rage, disillusion and desperation when she turns to the church at a Christmas Eve midnight mass. But instead of finding salvation, she is beset by cruel flashbacks. In the ultimate act of resignation, believing now that nothing can save her from her own misery, not even God, she takes a paracetamol overdose.

It's all played out with a depth we seldom see on British television. McClure's wholesale acceptance of the character and what she is facing is so meticulously and thoughtfully delivered that we are left wounded and desperate to help, our frustration mounting, knowing we can only sit staring at our screens watching this mother and survivor of abuse and circumstance move from bad to worse. But in McClure's portrayal, we never get the feeling that this character is simply a victim. She has suffered at the hands of an evil predator, certainly, but is capable of clawing herself back from the brink, becoming a strong and supportive sister to Kelly and a stabilizing influence in the lives of Woody and younger members of the gang as the series progresses.

Another unique portrayal of a woman's survival comes in the Adrian Shergold-directed *Funny Cow* (2017). Starring Maxine Peake in the title role, the film was set in and around the northern working men's club circuit and detailed the life of a female protagonist who uses stand-up comedy in an attempt to make sense out of her troubled background and homelife. Though the premise may sound familiar, or whiff of a 'northern lass makes good' cliché, it's an effective yet sombre set piece that challenges stereotypes and romantic depictions of class, preferring instead to present us with an unpredictable and highly original non-linear story which defies easy representation in favour of something more real and urgent. And it's clear from an interview in Deirdre O'Neill's documentary *The Acting Class* that Peake is passionate about her class and background:

> … be honest, any great cultural movement as far as I'm concerned has always started from working-class culture and then the middle classes come and nick it, stick a price tag on it and then we have to pay a lot of money for it.

Peake's character, known only as 'Funny Cow' throughout the film, echoes these sentiments when she berates her middle-class lover (Paddy Considine) for being unable to see how Shakespeare and the theatre have been yanked from the reach of working-class people and earmarked by the affluent few. The character goes from childhood neglect and domestic abuse to queen of the cabaret — her own distinct brand of comedy being heavily influenced by the late Sheffield-born entertainer Marti Caine. And yet this is not the run-of-the-mill rise to glory, rags to riches tale where everything comes good in the end. There is no sense of anyone gaining true happiness throughout the film.

> Happiness comes and goes. I can't walk round grinning like a Cheshire cat, I'm just not like that.

This is more about one person's victory (of sorts) over mounting difficulty — a troubled past, a dysfunctional present and the deep-set misogyny inherent in the 70s club scene and wider society. But there is nothing about *Funny Cow*, or indeed Peake's excellent performance, which feels as though we are treading old ground. The story is cut up and thrown at us in a non-chronological order; we shift from childhood to early adult life to the present and back with no clear explanation, the unconventional presentation perhaps reflecting Funny Cow's slightly off-kilter way of seeing the world. She is the embodiment of both strength and fragility. These two warring factions clash in her self-deprecating yet savage brand of stand-up, inspired by morose mentor Lenny (Alun Armstrong).

> We aren't twinned with anywhere but we do have a suicide pact with Mansfield.

It is also an unflinchingly real portrait of 70s Britain, with its grottiness, broken glass and dog-shit littered streets. The clubs we are invited into are dark, smoky, godless dives, where one might find stardom or a defeated old comedian hanging from a toilet chain in a urine-stinking punchline.

Funny Cow's red attire which she dons in many of the film's scenes — from childhood scarlet coat and tights, to the sparkly outfit she wears on stage, is a bloody visual reminder of femininity, an angry act of disobedience. Like the character's personality it also acts as red rag to a bull — as though her very presence is challenging to that era's environment. It may be subtler but it's as defiant in intent as Billy Casper's two fingered salute.

Within the narrative, she not only challenges the ideas of her sexist male contemporaries and clubland gate-keepers, she also challenges our own cosy ideas of the past and the northern club scene, which have been wrapped in twenty-first-century waves of nostalgia.

Though the northern club scene may have thrown up many stars who have fallen into modern legend and post-millennial acceptance, such as Tommy Cooper, Jim Bowen, Roy Walker, Frank Carson and Marti Caine, this film never shies away from what is definitely, through modern eyes, the unacceptable side of that circuit.

A star like Bernard Manning is often used as a poster child for that aggressively old-school form of comedy that was given a serious kicking in the early 80s alternative wave. It was built largely on homophobia, sexism and racism, and it is clear that Manning's own insidious form of knockabout prejudice, which away from the TV cameras could devolve from non-PC humour into out-and-out hatred, was incredibly popular. And given that he rose to fame in an era of Enoch Powell, and primetime TV shows like *The Black and White Minstrel Show*, it's not entirely surprising. But the man was hardly alone, casual and not-so-casual racism, and certainly jokes about 'poofs', were endemic within that culture. And yet what is often forgotten is that these comics were finely-tuned professionals, they had perfected timing and technique in sometimes in the direst of circumstances — the club circuit could be very unforgiving.

I recently re-watched a few episodes of old ITV show *The Comedians*, which rode high in the weekend schedules for a number of years in the 70s and early 80s. Its regular roster of stand-ups included Mike Reid, Mick Miller, Stan Boardman and Bernard Manning. The racism and prejudice of the era was certainly present, there was no shortage of the kinds of dodgy material mentioned previously. I am in no sense making any excuses for that, but what there also was, was a surprising and often-forgotten elevated level of storytelling and ingenuity. These comics were well-trained joke machines.

It is the level of storytelling — the ability to capture the attention and use the imagination, to paint narratives, which has long been the tradition of the working classes, who are usually denied the more academic routes of the more affluent middle and upper echelons of society. As Peake herself offers: 'I just think that people have a really dim view of working class and working-class culture… How we are as people, our educational abilities, but I just think we need to tell stories to progress in order to understand each other…'

It is the bringing together of all these elements, the craftsmanship of storytelling, the humour and yes, the homophobia and racism of the 70s club circuit, which makes the film and the character of *Funny Cow* so unflinchingly real and engaging.

Though *Funny Cow* may have been aimed (at least via its marketing) at the kind of audiences who flocked to films such as *Made in Dagenham* (2010), *The Full Monty* (1997) or even *Billy Elliot* (2000), I feel it offers something much more authentic, darker and deeper than any of those more 'feel-good' dramas. There is nothing in *Funny Cow* which panders, like the title character the film is uncompromising, surprising, utterly watchable and ultimately fascinating.

17: Modern Times

Whatever happens up there, you are on your own.

Jawbone (2017)

This book began with a look at the career of Charlie Chaplin. Chaplin, originally from South London, made a living playing a homeless figure on the fringes of society. In one of his finest moments, in *City Lights*, his tramp character is pitted against a seemingly unbeatable enemy with no escape from the confines of a blood-soaked boxing ring. So it seems fitting that I should conclude this book with a look at a much more recent film which also features a South Londoner playing a homeless man on the edges of society, who is thrust back into the boxing ring.

Jawbone (2017), directed by Thomas Napper and written by and starring Johnny Harris, is one of a raft of 'thinking man's boxing films' to have been released this century. Stateside entries have included the Jake Gyllenhaal vehicle, *Southpaw* (2015), and the earlier *Cinderella Man* (2005), while a recent British take on this sub-genre, Paddy Considine's stark and emotional road-to-recovery movie, *Journeyman* (2017), has garnered much critical acclaim and proved popular with the arthouse crowd.

But *Jawbone* simply belongs in this book more than any other. Not only is it a superb film, it also resonates on a deeper level and seems to chime perfectly with the nature and main thrust of this body of work, and it provides a handy close to the narrative.

While it's true that *Jawbone* is a deeply personal story, at least parts of it being almost semi-autobiographical, it is more than that. It does not relate a tale which may or may not be based on certain facts, what it does more than anything, is provide us with an unquestionable truth.

Jimmy, the film's protagonist, immaculately handled by Harris, who manages to exude both darkness and humanity, appears to be out of luck. Having recently lost his mother, he finds himself out on the streets when he refuses the chance of alternative accommodation when his late parent's flat is condemned by the council. Struggling with alcohol addiction, without a roof over his head, he returns to the one place which once gave him a purpose in life, his local boxing gym.

At first, Jimmy returns to the gym sheepishly, avoiding eye contact. This is Harris at his shadowy, lonely best, able to lurk in dark corners even where there are no dark corners. It soon becomes clear that although there was once a bond between him and gym owner Bill, brilliantly underplayed by Ray Winstone, the bond has been fractured somewhat by Jimmy's descent into alcoholism.

Agreeing to lay off the booze, Jimmy is reluctantly welcomed back into the gym — 'If I find one bottle of booze in 'ere and you're out. You understand?' A troubled relationship develops between Jimmy and dedicated but tough trainer Eddie (Michael Smiley). Eddie is unable to be as forgiving of Jimmy's past misdemeanours as Bill.

But when Jimmy inadvisably enters himself in an illegal boxing bout arranged by creepy gangster Joe (Ian McShane), the two are thrown together. The relationship, though troubled, strengthens after Bill loses his battle with cancer and the fight draws closer.

The fight itself, when we get to it, is brutally realised. Though Harris is a master player when it comes to understatement, this is his most physical performance. An ex-boxer himself, Harris brought in Barry McGuigan as an advisor to supervise training sessions and ensure the fight was as authentic as possible. Jimmy, thrown into the ring with a younger, bigger opponent, takes a punishing battering, and it's an uneasy watch. Drained of any Hollywood romanticism, it's messy, visceral and unpleasant. We hear the baying animalistic crowd, feel each illegal blow, our cosy sensibilities knocked out of the skull. The sequence is not so much played out as spat upon the screen through swollen bloodied lips. And as with other screen boxing bouts, this is not simply a case of who will be the winner or loser, the stakes are higher than that, not just in terms of the substantial purse Jimmy stands to gain, but there is every possibility that one of them will not make it out of the ring alive. It's a brilliantly tense piece of filmmaking, expertly captured by director Napper and cinematographer Tat Radcliffe. As viewers we simply cannot call the outcome, it could go anywhere, and we are given no easy clues as to how this story will play out.

And yet *Jawbone* is undoubtedly a cerebral film. Jimmy's main battle is not so much with a bloodthirsty opponent as with himself. The film, though never spilling into saccharine territory, is deeply emotional and the struggle presented to us is certainly an internal one, a heavyweight brawl with grief and a fragile control over debilitating addiction. The film's heart and Jimmy's predicament is perhaps never more clearly depicted than when he is shown sitting alone on a bench in the dead of night gazing into the blood-black waters of the Thames, desperately trying not to drink the bottle of vodka which is stashed away in its hiding place, gnawing at his soul.

From Chaplin through to *Love on the Dole*, the British New Wave, *Kes*, *Funny Cow* and beyond, I hope I have at least touched upon some important films, themes and people. As stated in the introduction, this book was never meant to be an academic or in-depth historical narrative. The features which I have discussed here are, I believe, crucial in the development of British film and its relationship with the system at hand. In an age where class is often left off the table during vital conversations about oppression, prejudice or inequality, it is the elephant in the room few political commentators wish to address or even acknowledge. I think these films shine a light on many issues or lives that would otherwise be ignored.

But like Jimmy staring into the river or Arthur Seaton gazing into the mirror or even the Little Tramp shuffling into the sunset, it's difficult to know how this story will continue. The working classes have often, as I hope I've shown in this book, been presented fairly and evenly in the many fascinating films I have talked about, and yet with the continuing televisual obsession with demonising those on lower incomes via shows like *On Benefits and Proud* or *Saints and Scroungers*, which set out to reduce complicated lives into easily-swallowed stereotypes, it's always going to be an uphill battle.

What working-class people are good at is telling stories, and film can be an excellent way of either capturing or presenting those stories. Twenty-first-century offerings such as *Jawbone*, *Tyrannosaur*, *I, Daniel Blake* or even *This is England* have shown us these stories are not going to go away and that working-class cinema is not just about the black-and-white visions of the past. These stories will endure in one form or another. And hopefully modern filmmakers, writers and actors will continue to make sure that the working classes control their own narrative.

Ta for reading this. I hope it's all been worth it.

> *I could understand it if it was money, but chuff me, a book?*
>
> *Kes*

Select Bibliography

Books

Ackroyd, P. (2014) *Charlie Chaplin*, Chatto and Windus, London.

Anderson, L. (2005) *The Diaries*, Methuen, London.

Braine, J. (1957) *Room at the Top*, Arrow Books, London.

Caine, M. (2010) *The Elephant to Hollywood*, Hodder and Stoughton, London.

Chaplin, C. (1964) *My Autobiography*, The Bodley Head Ltd., London.

Cousins, M. (2004) *The Story of Film*, Pavilion Books, London.

Dewe Mathews, T. (1994) *Censored*, Chatto and Windus, London.

Durgnat, R. (2011) *A Mirror for England: British Movies from Austerity to Affluence* (2nd edition), Palgrave Macmillan, London.

Gillet, P. (2003) *The British Working Class in Post War Film*, Manchester University Press, Manchester.

Hancock, F and Nathan, D. (1969) *Hancock*, Coronet, London.

Hayward, A. (2004) *Which Side are You on?* Bloomsbury Publishing PLC, London.

King, G. (2002) *Film Comedy*, Wallflower Press, London.

Leigh, M. (1994) *Naked and Other Screenplays*, Faber and Faber, London.

Pirie, D. (2008) *A New Heritage of Horror: The English Gothic Cinema*, I.B. Taurus, London.

Poitier, S. (2000) *The Measure of a Man*, Harper Collins, New York.

Sillitoe, A. (1958) *Saturday Night and Sunday Morning* (3rd edition), Pan Books Ltd., London.

Smith, J. (1984) *Chaplin*, Columbus Books, London.

Walker, A. (1985) *National Heroes: British Cinema in the Seventies and Eighties*, Orion Books Ltd, London.

Watson, G. (2004) *The Cinema of Mike Leigh*, Wallflower Press, London.

Articles and Interviews

Ashley Clarke, (updated 16 August 2018) *10 Great Black British Films*, The BFI, accessed 15 January 2019.

<https://www.bfi.org.uk/news-opinion/news-bfi/lists/10-great-black-british-films>

Mark Duguid (2003-2014), *The Long Good Friday*, The BFI, accessed 15 January 2018
<http://www.screenonline.org.uk/film/id/444789/index.html>

Christoph Dupin (2003-2014), The BFI, 2 April 2018
<http://www.screenonline.org.uk/film/id/444789/index.html>

Kermode Uncut (2012) [Blog] Directed by Nick Frend Jones. UK: BBC

A Conversation with Robert Buchanan (2014) Produced by Douglas Weir. UK: BFI

The Acting Class (2017) [DVD] Directed by Deirdre O'Neill and Mike Wayne. UK: Inside Film Network

Filmography

How Bridget Served the Salad Undressed (1898)
From the Manger to the Cross (1912)
The Bank (1915)
The Tramp (1915)
The Floorwalker (1916)
The Fireman (1916)
Easy Street (1917)
The Immigrant (1917)
The Cabinet of Doctor Caligari (1920)
The Kid (1921)
Nosferatu (1922)
The Gold Rush (1925)
Battleship Potemkin (1925)
The Jazz Singer (1927)
The Circus (1928)
City Lights (1931)
Freaks (1932)
Island of Lost Souls (1932)
The Mad Doctor (1933)
It Happened One Night (1934)
The Bride of Frankenstein (1935)
Modern Times (1936)
The Lady Vanishes (1938)
The Great Dictator (1940)
Love on the Dole (1941)
In Which We Serve (1942)
The Wicked Lady (1945)
The Seventh Veil (1945)
The Dead of Night (1946)
The Bells of St Mary's (1946)
The Jolson Story (1946)
Holiday Camp (1947)
It Always Rains on Sunday (1947)
Brighton Rock (1948)
Bicycle Thieves (1948)
The Wooden Horse (1950)
Pool of London (1951)

O Dreamland (1953)
On the Waterfront (1954)
The Quatermass Xperiment (1955)
Blackboard Jungle (1955)
The Night of the Hunter (1955)
Rebel Without a Cause (1955)
The Bespoke Overcoat (1956)
The Curse of Frankenstein (1957)
Dracula (1958)
The Defiant Ones (1958)
The Mummy (1959)
Carry On Nurse (1959)
We Are the Lambeth Boys (1959)
Look Back in Anger (1959)
Room at the Top (1959)
Tiger Bay (1959)
Pollyanna (1960)
The Entertainer (1960)
Carry On Constable (1960)
Saturday Night and Sunday Morning (1960)
The Curse of the Werewolf (1961)
A Taste of Honey (1961)
Whistle Down the Wind (1961)
Flame in the Streets (1961)
To Kill a Mockingbird (1962)
The Intruder (1962)
The L-Shaped Room (1962)
The Loneliness of the Long Distance Runner (1962)
A Kind of Loving (1962)
Dr. No (1962)
This Sporting Life (1963)
Billy Liar (1963)
Carry On Cabby (1963)
A Hard Day's Night (1964)
Up the Junction (1965)
Cathy Come Home (1966)
The Plague of the Zombies (1966)
Alfie (1966)
Poor Cow (1967)